BEFORE THE SABBATH

A  BOOK

Books by Eric Hoffer

ERIC HOFFER

BEFORE
THE SABBATH

1817

HARPER & ROW, PUBLISHERS

NEW YORK, HAGERSTOWN

SAN FRANCISCO

LONDON

FIRST EDITION

Designed by Sidney Feinberg

Library of Congress Cataloging in Publication Data

Hoffer, Eric.
  Before the Sabbath.
  (A Cass Canfield book)
  I. Title.
AC8.H7317 1979   081   78–69626
ISBN 0–06–011914–4

79 80 81 82 83 10 9 8 7 6 5 4 3 2 1

To Charlie Kittrell,
with much affection

BEFORE THE SABBATH

November 26, 1974, 10:00 P.M.

The other day I finished the first draft of a slim collection of short essays. I suddenly had the feeling that I had been scraping the bottom of the barrel, and that the slim volume might mark my end as a thinker. I doubted whether I would ever get involved in a new, seminal train of thought. It was legitimate to assume that at the age of seventy-two my mind was played out.

I did not panic. As a retired workingman I now have the right to do what I have denied myself since 1940—read novels; thousands of them. There are only a few years left anyhow. But first I have to get a clear picture of the manner in which age affects my mind. The reasoning capacity is unimpaired. I can still tell sense from nonsense, and my judgment of books I am reading and of my own writing is sound. It is true that I have noticed a tendency toward wishful thinking, a lessened interest in what is happening in the world, and a marked weakening of memory. But I sense that the crucial difference lies elsewhere, in the loss of alertness.

I remembered something I wrote in *Reflections on the Human Condition:* "That which is unique and worthwhile in us makes itself felt only in flashes. If we do not know how to catch and savor the flashes we are without growth and exhilaration." Would it be possible to reanimate and cultivate the alertness to the first, faint stirrings of thought? What would happen if I forced myself over a period of several months to sluice my mind the way I sluiced dirt in my gold-hunting days, using

1

a diary as a sluicebox to trap whatever flakes of insight might turn up?

This, then, is why I am starting this diary today. I intend to keep it for at least six months, and I have promised my weary mind a blissful Sabbath when the task is done.

November 27, 7:30 A.M.

The democracies are entering 1975 without confidence in the future. They are paralyzed by fear when facing external or internal adversaries. There is not a democracy that dares say boo to the pack of oil sheiks who are pushing the free world into recession and stagnation. It may seem that the Russian presence keeps the Western democracies from forceful action. Actually, the fear of opposition at home outweighs the fear of intervention by the Russian Mediterranean fleet. Adversary intellectuals and alienated youths are likely to explode in the streets should a democracy try to secure by force the flow of oil at a reasonable price. There seems to be no possibility at present of a strong government in a free country. And it seems preposterous that the loss of confidence and paralysis of will were caused by the barrage of words coming from adversary intellectuals.

8:00 P.M.   In the West the disenchantment of the better educated with their homeland is a fairly recent phenomenon. In this country it first surfaced in the 1930s, faded during the 1940s and 1950s, but came back in full force in the 1960s.

Strangely, the prototype of this disenchantment is the attitude of the Russian intelligentsia toward the Czarist regime during the second half of the nineteenth century. Many members of that intelligentsia saw Russian history as a progression from one tyranny to another and longed for a wholly new beginning. It staggers the mind that intellectuals living off the fat of the land in a fairly free America should feel as oppressed and trapped as did intellectuals in Czarist Russia.

2

November 28, 7:30 A.M.

A letter from Eric* yesterday. The hard work of planting trees on the cold mountains justifies his existence, hardens his body, and seems to stimulate his mind. Here is a striking example of the double function of work in our society: to do what needs to be done, and to give the worker a sense of usefulness. In the case of a young workingman hard work gives a sense of manliness, and the earned money an exhilarating feeling of independence.

9:30 P.M.   I find myself wondering about Peter Viereck and Stuart Hughes, two excellent writers who have not of late appeared in print. They are probably younger than I am. How good it would be if one could stop writing in old age without feeling diminished. Shakespeare did it. Would the world lose much were there an established custom of writers' ceasing to write at sixty-five?

One of the surprising privileges of intellectuals is that they are free to be scandalously asinine without harming their reputation. The intellectuals who idolized Stalin while he was purging millions and stifling the least stirring of freedom have not been discredited. They are still holding forth on every topic under the sun and are listened to with deference. Sartre returned in 1939 from Germany, where he studied philosophy, and told the world that there was little to choose between Hitler's Germany and France. Yet Sartre went on to become an intellectual pope revered by the educated in every land. The metaphysical grammarian Noam Chomsky, who went to Hanoi to worship there at the altar of human rights and democ-

---

* Eric Osborne. He and his brother Steven, who were children when I wrote *Working and Thinking on the Waterfront,* are young men now. When this was written, Steven and his wife, Beatrice, were living in San Francisco, not far from the home of Steven's and Eric's mother, Lili Osborne. Eric was working in Oregon.

3

racy, was not discredited and silenced when the humanitarian communists staged their nightmare in South Vietnam and Cambodia. Is there a greater freedom than the right to be wrong?

The Nixon tragedy: A man of unsurpassed courage and outstanding intelligence but without vision. An opportunist who missed his greatest opportunity. He had the chance to mobilize the free world's science and technological know-how to find, in ten years or so, a new source of cheap, clean energy. He could have set in motion a concerted effort to rehabilitate a polluted and depleted continent, renovate decayed cities, and in the process give the young who now pack the cities unlimited opportunities for useful action. He could have become the symbol of an era in which human rather than natural resources are the wellspring of wealth, vigor and greatness.

November 29, 7:00 A.M.
    I cannot see myself living in a socialist society. My passion is to be left alone and only a capitalist society does so. Capitalism is ideally equipped for mastering things but awkward in mastering men. It hugs the assumption that people will perform tolerably well when left to themselves.
    The curious thing is that the reluctance or inability to manage men makes capitalist society uniquely modern. Managing men is a primitive thing. It partakes of magic and is the domain of medicine men and tribal chieftains. Socialist and communist societies are a throwback to the primitive in their passion for managing men.
    Idealists never weary of decrying capitalism for its trivial motivation. Yet a discrepancy between trivial motives and weighty consequences is an essential trait of human uniqueness and is particularly pronounced in the creative individual. Not only in the marketplace and on the battlefield but also in the world of thought and imagination, men who set their hearts on toys often accomplish great things. The idealists prize seri-

ousness and weightiness. Let them go to the animal kingdom!
Animals are deadly serious.

November 30, 6:00 A.M.
I am reading *The Lunatic Express* by Charles Miller.
The author is a professional writer who was asked by a publisher
to write the story of the Uganda railroad built by the British
in the middle decades of the nineteenth century. The story
is told extremely well. Months ago, while writing the essay
"Black Studies" for the new book, I read all I could about
the Arab slave traders. Miller's book retells much that is familiar
to me, yet I enjoy reading it. The early chapters are about
Zanzibar and the slave trade. One impression: the stench rising
from the dark continent. He refers to Zanzibar as Stinkibar.
The world must have stunk through much of history.
Reading about nineteenth-century Uganda one realizes that
Idi Amin is not an anomaly. Many of Uganda's rulers (the Kaba-
kas) were clowning tyrants, "degenerates, liars, sadists."

5:30 P.M.   I have a hunch that the Arabs will use
their oil billions not to modernize their countries but to redress
the balance between the Christian West and the Islamic East.
They are financing the pressure against the non-Moslem en-
claves of Lebanon, Israel and Ethiopia. Idi Amin is a Moslem
hero kept in power by Arab money in largely Christian Uganda.
Moslems are also gaining the upper hand in the republic of
Chad and in Nigeria. The Islamization of Africa is a dream
to fire Arab hearts.

December 1, 7:45 A.M.
In 1958 a director of industry and commerce in the
Indian state of Andhra Pradesh complained that in India it
would be easier to launch a satellite than provide people with
food, clothing and shelter. The same was true of Russia. Things
were different in the advanced democracies. However, in 1974,

a British director of industry and commerce could complain that in Britain it is easier to make scientific and technological discoveries, easier even to write great books and compose great music, than induce workers to exert themselves in factories and mines.

I wonder what would happen should Britain become wholly socialist. Science can thrive in non-capitalist countries, but I doubt whether writers and artists will produce anything great where they are not left alone to stew in their own juice. The fact that in communist Russia the cultural intelligentsia feels more important and socially useful than in capitalist countries has not released a marked creative flow. A state monopoly of publishing and censorship by the noncreative have turned Russia into a cultural wasteland. Probably what the creative spirit needs is an annoyance that irritates but does not crush. Russia under an inefficient Czarist tyranny became a nursery of great writers, composers and scientists.

December 2, 8:00 A.M.

It is almost eight years since I retired from the waterfront, but in my dreams I still load and unload ships. I sometimes wake up in the morning aching all over from a night's hard work. One might maintain that a pension is pay for the work we keep on doing in our dreams after we retire.

I am inclined to think that at present it is the inefficient societies that are likely to be more stable. By inefficient I mean societies that employ as many workers as possible to do a job. Such societies have a wide distribution of a sense of usefulness, which is more vital to the maintenance of social stability than the distribution of wealth or power.

December 3, 4:00 P.M.

A world that did not lift a finger when Hitler was wiping out six million Jewish men, women and children is now saying that the Jewish state of Israel will not survive if it does not come to terms with the Arabs. My feeling is that no one in this universe has the right and the competence to tell Israel what it has to do in order to survive. On the contrary, it is Israel that can tell us what to do. It can tell us that we shall not survive if we do not cultivate and celebrate courage, if we coddle traitors and deserters, bargain with terrorists, court enemies and scorn friends.

December 4, 7:00 A.M.

The Chinese Far East (which includes Japan, Korea, Vietnam and Mongolia) is at present the last refuge of the work ethic. In the rest of the world labor faking is the rule. It matters not whether a country is feudal, capitalist, socialist, communist, backward or advanced, rich or poor, its people will do as little as possible. Here is a description of the situation in Russia: "At any time, in any office, 80 percent of the staff is in the corridors or the bathrooms. No one works." Something similar is taking place in capitalist societies. The fateful event of our time is not the advancement of backward countries but the leveling down of advanced countries.

I am curious about Pechorin, a Russian intellectual of the mid-nineteenth century who wrote a poem on "How sweet it is to hate one's native land and eagerly await its annihilation." Pechorin became a Catholic and ended his days as a monk in a monastery. In a letter to Alexander Herzen he predicted that "the material civilization will lead to a tyranny from which there will be no shelter." He thought that a greedy bourgeoisie would sell its soul for material rewards. Actually, the logic of events has been more subtle. Our materialist civilization is edging toward tyranny because the elimination of scarcity also eliminates the hidden hand of circumstances that kept the wheels turning. The coming of abundance has weakened social automatism and discipline. Societies now need forceful authority in order to function tolerably well.

December 5, 6:30 A.M.

We should have been on the lookout for the snake to pop up when we were given a taste of paradisiacal affluence. And, remembering that the snake was "more subtle [hence more learned] than any beast in the field," we might have guessed that he would come out of the universities.

It is now the fashion to contrast authority with human rights. But we are learning that the moment authority becomes ineffectual most of our rights are nullified by the many-headed tyranny of anarchy.

December 6, 7:00 A.M.

There is a large body of educated opinion that wants to see white humanity diminished and defeated. Would an Africa cleansed of white men be a better place for black men to live in? We hear glib talk about the predicament of a Negro living in a white society. Yet in Africa and elsewhere it is the misery of Negroes living in a Negro world that demands attention.

The decline of nationalism in the Occident after the Second World War gave rise to two opposite tendencies. When it no longer seemed so glorious to be an Englishman, a Frenchman, a German, it became more attractive to be a European or a member of an Atlantic community. But it also became more attractive to be reborn as a Scotsman, Welshman, Breton, Burgundian. The weakening of nationalism increased the readiness for international affiliation but also released an impulse toward ethnic separatism.

The proponents of change claim that they aim to make society more responsive to what people want. Actually, what people want most is stability and continuity rather than change.

December 7, 5:00 A.M.

A revulsion from work is a fundamental component of human nature. It is natural to feel work to be a curse. A social order that grants only minimal necessities but asks for little effort will be more stable than a system that offers superfluities but demands ceaseless striving. One reason communist governments seem so stable is that they no longer insist on hard work. Islam too is markedly stable because it functions tolerably well in an atmosphere of indolence.

In the period between the two World Wars Czechoslovakia was one of the most progressive and prosperous countries in Europe. It had an industrious, skilled population that kept the economic and social plant in good repair. In 1948 the communists took over, and twenty years later, when the lid came off during the Dubcek interlude, the world could see the changes that had taken place under communist rule. The chief change was the loss of the work ethic. The Czechoslovaks took to labor faking with gusto. Hard work was looked upon as a violation of the fraternal code. It was also startling to discover how easily the workers had adjusted themselves to a lower standard of living. It seemed doubtful whether an offer of higher wages could wean them from their meager brand of *la dolce vita*.

In Britain workers are immune to the blandishments of a higher living standard, and this attitude is spreading to other democracies, particularly among the young. I suspect that the present chatter about quality of life is an attempt to mask the fact that to the new generation the good life is a life of little effort.

December 8, 7:00 A.M.

How strange the nineteenth century! It was a century in which ceaseless, drastic change went hand in hand with a strong sense of continuity—even of immutability. There was a widespread assumption that prevailing patterns would persist

9

indefinitely. Even the people who dreamed wild dreams and foresaw apocalyptic dénouements lived regular, stable lives.

Nowhere and at no time have people of all sorts become rich so quickly as in Britain during the first half of the nineteenth century. Rapid industrialization not only opened fabulous opportunities for enrichment to the middle classes, but the landowning aristocrats had more than their share of the explosion of prosperity. It was this unprecedented outburst of moneymaking that gave Britain's ruling class its confidence during a time of drastic change.

December 9, 8:00 A.M.

When Americans do not act the way I think they ought to, my reaction depends on whether I feel one of them or see myself as an outsider. When I feel one of them I tend to accuse them of cowardice, gullibility, mindless conformity and the like. But as an outsider I wonder whether the reason Americans do not act the way I expect them to is that they "know" more. I am aware that I lack their social instincts and skills. Their forbearance and patience derive from their deep-seated belief that given time situations work themselves out.

The change that matters is the change of a society's axioms. The 1960s saw a slaughter of axioms. It would be interesting to identify the new axioms. I can think of a couple: (1) The object of life is fun. (2) The world owes everyone a living.

December 10, 7:45 A.M.

I have always felt depleted in December. I remember how twenty years ago I ate my heart out all through December trying to write an article on the intellectual and the masses for *The Pacific Spectator*. It was the first time I undertook to write something to order. It seemed disastrous that I had to do the writing in December. Yet that article turned out to be one of the better things I had done.

December 11, 8:20 A.M.

The role of immigrants in the life of the modern Occident: The churning of population in the wake of the Reformation had an energizing effect on Germany, Holland and England. The wave of overseas migration during the nineteenth century not only was a factor in the development of America but was also responsible for the prolonged internal stability in Europe during the soul-wrenching changes brought about by the industrial revolution.

What will be the effect of the present influx of foreign workers into Europe? It will reinforce the revulsion of West European workers from hard, monotonous and dirty jobs. It may also, by turning peasants into mechanics, accelerate the modernization of the backward countries (Turkey, Yugoslavia, Portugal, Algeria) the foreign workers come from.

The fact that European countries cannot assimilate foreign workers underlines America's uniqueness and newness.

December 12, 3:00 P.M.

Kemal Atatürk knew that Islam is incompatible with modernization. He deliberately tried to uproot Islam by laicizing everyday life and banishing Arab influences. He persecuted Islam with a personal passion.

Has he succeeded? Today, almost forty years after Atatürk's death, Islam is gaining ground in Turkey. It is apparently easier to de-Christianize than to de-Islamize. Islam's rapid and total de-Christianization of the Middle East and North Africa contrasts with the ineffectuality of Christian proselytizing in Islamic lands. Islam caters to basic human needs and is without inner contradictions and tensions. It legitimizes an easygoing,

11

even indolent life. I doubt whether any Islamic country can be durably modernized.

December 13, 10:20 A.M.

I say to myself: Lenin and Stalin between them liquidated at least sixty million Russians in order to build factories and dams. America welcomed thirty million immigrants to help build factories and dams.

Capitalism is fueled by the individual's appetites, ambitions, fears, hopes and illusions. Communism forces people to hate what they love and love what they hate. Imagine a country of land-hungry peasants forced to renounce ownership of land. Imagine a system that frowns on friendship, free association and individual enterprise. It is no wonder that after sixty years the Russian communist party must still coerce, suspect and minutely regulate the Russian people.

Can anyone visualize the time when the unemployed of a western Europe made stagnant by a shortage of energy and raw materials would storm the borders of Russia, where there is no unemployment, the way thousands of unemployed Mexicans are risking their lives to steal into capitalist America? Should the unlikely happen and communist Russia become truly prosperous, it will still have to guard its borders to prevent Russians from running away.

We are underestimating the passion of common people for freedom. We see every day common people doing their utmost to escape from nonfree to free countries.

December 14, 9:15 A.M.

We are surrounded by mysteries: the mystery of the absence of outstanding leaders anywhere on this planet; the mystery of teachers no longer able to teach children to read and write; the mystery of the blurring of differences between men and women—in San Francisco even a close look does not always tell you beyond doubt the sex of a person; the mystery of a majority incapable of getting angry with those who trample it underfoot.

No other century has seen so great a waste of young lives as we have seen with our eyes—not only in the two World Wars but in the 1960s. The twentieth century seems a crazed monstrous beast devouring its young.

I must try to make sense of the contrast between the nineteenth and the twentieth century. Have there ever been two successive centuries so different from each other?

The day before he died, Renoir painted anemones with a brush strapped to his crippled fingers. When he finished, he said: "I am beginning to learn how to paint anemones."

On his deathbed Michelangelo said to Cardinal Salivati: "I regret that I die just as I am beginning to learn the alphabet of my profession."

I cannot see a writer saying toward the end of his life that he is just beginning to learn how to write. A writer never knows he can write the way a painter knows he can paint or a sculptor knows he can sculpt or even a composer knows he can compose. Not long before his death Adam Smith observed that after all his practice in writing he composed as slowly and with as much difficulty as he had at first. V. S. Pritchett sees it as "one of the disgusts of the writer's life that he finds himself having to learn from the beginning again every time he puts pen to paper."

December 15, 10:00 A.M.

Through most of history laborers must have lived soul-emptying lives. The Greeks did not believe a laborer could think, let alone contemplate beauty. Yet men have sung as they worked from the beginning of time. Work has its ancestry in play.

According to the Bible God placed Adam in the Garden of

13

Eden "to dress it and keep it." It was pleasant, playful work. With the expulsion from Eden man came face to face with hard, monotonous, endless work.

Disraeli was certain there is no greater misfortune than to have a heart that will not grow old. Actually, when we have someone we dearly love and who loves us a young heart is no misfortune. It reconciles us with the human species. The misanthropy of the old comes from the fading of the magic glow of desire.

December 16, 8:00 A.M.

Last night we had a happy time at Lili's house cooking, eating and then putting up the Christmas tree. It is amazing how easily my spirits revive when I am with people I love.

Why should not the Occident stop for a while—stop growing, working, consuming, wasting? The silenced machinery would be kept in good repair, and research continue as before. But life would be frugalized and simplified. Let the backward countries work and catch up! The Occident, for the first time in two centuries, would take time off to recharge its batteries.

December 17, 8:20 A.M.

Both the Hapsburg and the Ottoman empires dominated the Balkans for centuries. Yet in the Balkans today there is little left of the Austrian presence, while a number of towns in Macedonia and Serbia have Turkish mosques and retain the Turkish language. Could it be that the more foreign an influence, the more enduring its mark? The Turkish influence in the Balkans was the more foreign. Would the same hold true of British influence in India? The Turks intermarried more with their subjects than did the Austrians. But perhaps the persistence of Turkish influence is another instance of the persistence of Islam (December 12). Spain still shows strong traces of Islam seven centuries after its de-Islamization, whereas few signs of Christianity are left in Islamized North Africa.

10:45 P.M.   I went over by taxicab to meet Eric's train in Oakland and spent the whole day at Lili's house. Steven and Beatrice came over. We are, the five of us, a real family.

It seems preposterous that I who landed on Skid Row at the age of eighteen, and spent twenty years on the bum, one step ahead of hunger, should worry about Eric going out into a cold world at the age of nineteen. It is an instance of the truth that we tend to see those we love as brittle and vulnerable.

Eric is the only human being I have known from the word go. I shall always think of him as a child—perpetually vulnerable and inexperienced. I shall always tremble for his fate and fear the worst. Paradoxically, though I have watched Eric closely from the day he was born, I understand him less than I do others.

December 18, 7:15 A.M.
     I am reading the autobiography of Norman Bentwich, an English Jew. It has puzzled me that English Jewry has not produced until recently outstanding scientists, writers and artists. There has not been one English-born Jewish Nobel Prize winner. When you compare this with the accomplishments of Jews in Germany, France, Austria, Italy and America you feel that you are up against a seminal problem. Even Russia has produced two Jewish Nobel Prize winners—Pasternak and Landau.

England has been an ideal milieu for outsiders. Scotsmen, Irishmen, Australians, New Zealanders, Canadians, Americans and nationals from several European countries have been prominent in many fields. Jews excelled in business, manufacturing and to some extent in public life. England is perhaps the only Western country where Jews have not played a central role in the development of nuclear physics. Are there any famous Jewish names associated with Oxford and Cambridge? I can think only of Wittgenstein (an Austrian Jew), Sir Isaiah Berlin, and Max Beloff. My hunch is that Jews did not feel at ease in Oxford and Cambridge, where social intercourse is as vital as the process of learning.

Is there a difference in style between English and Jewish nuclear physics? Einstein's scientific thinking had a metaphysical undertone. He wanted to rethink God's thoughts. He felt that "behind all discernible concatenations there remains something subtle, intangible and inexplicable. Veneration for this force beyond anything we can comprehend is my religion." To Rutherford, the mysterious rays emitted from a substance were "the debris of decaying atoms."

December 19, 8:00 A.M.

I derive a peculiar pleasure from the fact that several of man's earliest achievements have remained unsurpassed: some cave paintings, the domesticated plants and animals, the storytelling of the Old Testament. It makes it seem almost natural that my first book should be my best. I am less confident now than when I began writing thirty years ago. All I can do now is wring a few drops of essence from a shrunken mind.

There is much in the Bentwich book about Palestine in the 1920s and '30s. The Arabs refused to coexist with the Jews even when they (the Arabs) had the upper hand. The backwardness of the Arabs in most fields of endeavor makes it impossible for them to acquire the confidence necessary for genuine cooperation with the Jews.

December 20, 7:45 A.M.

We had a fine time last night. Eric, barefoot in the kitchen, experimented with a mixture of calf's brains, figs and nuts. The mess did not taste good but we had plenty of baked chicken. I was high on Wild Turkey.

The other day I wondered how I would react if someone demonstrated to me beyond the least doubt that I am mean, deceitful, selfish and ruthless. The answer is: So long as there is a person I love and who loves me, and so long as I have some ability to think and write, I would go on uncrushed, accepting the fact that I am without the capacity to see myself as I am. I doubt whether I am capable of mortifying remorse. I might even quote St. Paul: "No one does good; not even one."

December 21, 6:30 A.M.

It comes as a surprise to find that Clausewitz saw a kinship between traders and warriors. In the essay on the trader in my new book I dwell on the interchange of roles between warriors and traders in the aftermath of the Second World War, when German and Japanese warriors became the world's foremost traders, and the Jews foremost warriors. I thought it was a new idea, but here is Clausewitz, a Prussian Junker, maintaining that the talents which make for success in business are similar to the talents of a successful military commander.

Early in the nineteenth century the Duke of Wellington objected to railways because "it would enable the lower orders to wander about the country escaping all proper control." In our time, the only person who might find it quite proper to make such a remark would be a high communist functionary. He would object to the introduction of an innovation that might enable people to "escape all proper control."

December 22, 6:45 A.M.

Bentwich felt at home wherever he went. There is hardly a complaint in the whole book. Hitler's holocaust is like a distant murmur. He remarks on "the fantastic orderliness of the German mind which caused them to keep a careful record of all their crimes." The allies found a card index of millions of names of victims. Clearly, the holocaust was accomplished not by psychopaths or maniacs but by ordinary, disciplined Germans, many of them clerks, who did a job and kept records.

We are eating out every night. I wanted it this way to save Lili the trouble of cooking and cleaning up. It also keeps us in a festive mood. This could be my last Christmas.

December 23, 7:30 A.M.
　　　　Communism was invented by highbrows while capitalism was initiated by lowbrows. A capitalist society can be run by anybody whereas it needs exceptional leaders to make a communist society work. If the vigor of an organization is measured by the ability to function well without an outstanding leader then, clearly, a communist society is less vigorous—less well made—than a capitalist society.
　　　　Churchill saw communist Russia ruled by a band of "bloody-minded professors." And, indeed, the contrast between a communist and a capitalist government is the contrast between a government by schoolmasters and a government by schoolboys. Churchill himself was one of the fabulous schoolboys who ruled Britain during the nineteenth century and up to the First World War. Apparently, lowbrows and schoolboys are better social builders than highbrows and schoolmasters.

Communism can reconstruct the chronically poor and launch backward countries on a road to modernization. Capitalism is ideal for enterprising, self-starting people but cannot do much for people who cannot help themselves. Clearly, where communism succeeds it makes the helpless fit for capitalism.

December 24, 7:45 A.M.
　　　　William McNeill's *The Shape of European History* has so far been a disappointment. The first two chapters, dealing

18

with theory, are pale and unimpressive. Some vague ideas about the nature of change. Not one sentence sticks in the mind. McNeill will be better when describing events and conveying information.

Despite its remarkable achievements in the Late Paleolithic (cave paintings) and Megalithic eras, Europe became a backward subcontinent during the Neolithic. Europe did not domesticate a single animal or plant, did not invent any sort of script, did not invent any thing comparable to the wheel, sail, or plow. Greece and Rome, though geographically part of Europe, were Mediterranean in spirit. Even their attitude toward Christianity was Mediterranean. Christianity did not create in Greece and Rome the tension of the soul which manifested itself in Europe when warrior tribes were made to adopt a religion of meekness and love.

McNeill asks: "What literature excels Homer, Aeschylus, Sophocles, Euripides?" I wonder whether these Greek masterpieces can engage the hearts and minds of people the way the literature of the Old Testament does. The storytelling of the Old Testament remains unmatched and it appeals not only to people of all climes and all walks of life but to children as well as adults.

My most vivid memories are of the middle twenty years of my life, 1920–1940. I was then on the bum and most of the time one step ahead of hunger. Those years seem to me eventful although life on the bum was actually endlessly repetitive. My stretched mind was exaggerating and fitting together slight happenings into fabulous, hilarious tales. And I was talking all the time, telling people about all that happened to me. They listened and roared with laughter. Sometimes when I came to a lumber camp or a work barrack people would ask me to tell them about my adventures. So in retrospect those twenty years are a procession of stories in which truth and fiction are so interwoven that I cannot tell them apart. I might almost say that I remember most minutely and distinctly things that did not happen to me.

19

December 25, 7:00 A.M.

 This year's Christmas is the happiest we have had. We shall have eleven people for breakfast and probably fifteen for dinner. The omens for the coming year are not favorable but we shall manage somehow.

 The historian Herbert Butterfield asks for "a more scientific analysis of the reasons why the twentieth century became an age of conflict." Could a scientific analysis explain why the Occident blundered into the First World War? There was nothing inevitable about the coming of the war and the terrible mess of its aftermath. Nor were Lenin's and Hitler's revolutions inevitable. How many people knew in 1914 that they were in the last year of a dying age?

 The great casualty of the First World War was hope. The belief in the perfectibility of man and the certainty of progress which began with the French Encyclopedists died with the war.

December 26, 6:45 A.M.

 There are evidently times when leaders do not appear no matter how urgent the need for them and how great the readiness to follow them. Right now the mess in Britain and Italy is crying out for a leader. The Occident will have to solve its problems without great leaders.

 It has been estimated that twelve million people were butchered, burned and tortured during the conversion of Mexico and Peru to Christianity. This was to an extent a recapitulation of what had taken place during the Christianization of Europe's pagans and heathens.

 When you compare Christianization with Romanization the contrast is staggering. The revival of Roman influence during the Renaissance must have been experienced by sensitive souls as a casting out of evil spirits.

The propagation of the communist faith in Russia exceeded Christianization in bloodletting and brutality. And there is no Russian Renaissance in sight to cast out the evil spirits.

December 27, 7:10 A.M.

I must stop smoking. It is wonderful how readily throat and lungs recuperate when I stop smoking for a while. Do animals recover as readily as human beings? My impression is that animals have no staying power once they sicken.

One could write a beautiful essay or even a small book on "The Flow of Influence."

The fact that the influence of the Occident is world-wide inclines us to assume that the flow of influence follows a hydraulic model; that it flows from high points of the human landscape to the low. We took it for granted until recently that the learned influence the ignorant, the advanced influence the backward, adults influence the young, and so on. It seemed natural that the Occident being more learned, advanced, rich and so on should influence the rest of the world. But we are no longer certain that it is so. At present, the children of the rich are adopting the attitudes, habits and even the language of low-class Negroes. Grownups are mimicking the fashions and the language of the young. The battle cries of backward countries are shaping the rhetoric of people in advanced countries. At first sight, this reversal of the flow of influence seems a demonstration of the topsy-turviness of our time. Actually, what we have here is a return to the past. The flow of influence followed a hydraulic model only for a short interval—after the coming of the industrial revolution. Up to A.D. 1800 the flow of influence was from the East to the West although the Occident had been pulling ahead since 1400. Through most of history it was the weak who influenced the strong. Not only did conquerors learn most readily from the conquered, but small countries most often shaped history. Israel, Greece and the small states of Italy gave the Occident its religion and the essential elements of its civilization. There is also the crucial fact that civilizations become most influential when they begin to decline. McNeill speaks of the cultural primacy which comes with economic decline as an "ecological succession": "The spread of classical Greek culture throughout the Mediterranean came after the economic power of Athens had broken down. Latin thought and letters penetrated the Western provinces of the Roman empire when Italy's economy was already in trouble." He adds that the influence of Moslem Spain and Byzantium became stronger "after military and economic disaster had struck the heartlands of both civilizations." It is also true that Italy's influence at the time of the Renaissance was at its height when Italian economic hegemony was in decline due to the self-assertion of native entrepreneurs in England, France, Germany, Spain and also in the Ottoman Empire.

Thus it is reasonable to assume that a decline of the Occident will not mean a diminution of its influence. On the contrary, the Occident's loss of military and economic supremacy will enhance its attractiveness as a model. Countries are most at ease when they imitate a defeated or dead model.

December 28, 6:45 A.M.

There is one more example of the link between material decline and increased cultural influence: the city of Vienna exerted its widest influence when it was the capital of a decaying Hapsburg empire.

In the past there were potential great leaders waiting in the wings. This was true of Hitler, Churchill, de Gaulle, Adenauer, Ben Gurion and others. Right now the wings are empty. Does the quality of the population have something to do with the absence of leaders? Hardly so. It is true that when there are leaders waiting in the wings their entrance onto the stage and their effectiveness depend on the character and attitudes of the people. Lenin knew his revolution was possible because of the inordinate submissiveness of the Russian people. Churchill had to wait for Dunkirk to prepare the British people for their finest hour. Hitler was possible only in Germany. De Gaulle did not get far because of the nature of the French.

I like to compare what Lenin said about the Russians with what de Gaulle said about the French. Lenin: "How can you compare the masses of Western Europe with our people—so patient, so accustomed to privation." De Gaulle: "What can you do with a country that has 315 different kinds of cheese?"

December 29, 9:45 A.M.
The current absence of outstanding leaders is so hard to explain that all guesses are legitimate. The women's liberation movement—the disenchantment of women with men—might be a factor. Women who worshiped them have often been prominent in the rise of great leaders.

About the flow of influence: Ghetto attitudes toward the law, work, and drugs were propagated by the universities. Students mimicked low-class Negroes, and non-students mimicked students. It reminds one of the spread of fashions in France: demimonde fashions were adopted by aristocratic ladies, and middle-class women mimicked the aristocrats.

When in the new book I advocate retirement at forty I ought to cite trenchant statistics. Workers over forty have to wait four times as long for new jobs as younger workers. In some countries two-thirds of the unemployed are over fifty. In short, when people pass forty they are in trouble if they have no firm base either in a strong union or in a special skill. I have the statistics from the *New York Times.* Yet I remember reading somewhere that in Britain young workers are so impossible that employers welcome the old. In some Welsh mines almost half of the miners are over fifty.

December 30, 7:50 A.M.
Back to the flow of influence: No foreign influence spread so rapidly and found such wholehearted acceptance as Romanization. Gaul was Romanized in less than fifty years.

The Roman way of life was embraced with ardor both in the East and in the West. It must have been breathtaking to see Roman cities spring out of the soil with their forums, colonnades, theatres and baths. Rome had a state-forming influence. Its success in influencing primitive people was due to its social effectiveness. Someone compared the two Celtic nations France and Ireland: France formed the first European state and Ireland the last, and the difference is due to the fact that Ireland had no Roman experience.

Greek influence was altogether different. The Greeks made an impact only on people with long-established civilizations. They had little effect on the Scythians, Illyrians and Thracians. The Greeks at Marseille had little influence on Celtic Gaul. Greek influence was largely esthetic and intellectual and was no factor in crystallizing and bolstering authority.

December 31, 8:00 A.M.

The nineteenth century despite its unprecedented changes was a century of law and order. In Britain, where the changes were most spectacular, the lower orders who early in the century had turned the cities into savage jungles became meek and law-abiding. The First World War was a watershed of effective authority in the Occident. In this country during the absorption of thirty million immigrants in the decades before the First World War, the cities were singularly peaceful and safe.

Was it the terrible slaughter and waste of the war that shook authority? Hardly so. It was the loss of hope. Hope unites people and induces patience. Hope was probably one of the most striking characteristics of Western humanity prior to the First World War. It was the loss of hope rather than its mere absence that drained authority of its effectiveness.

I suggested yesterday that Celtic Ireland was late in forming a state because it had no Roman experience. The same was true of Celtic Scotland and Wales. Yet the Irish, the Scotch and the Welsh played leading roles in the administration of Britain and its empire and also in the building of the United States. It is legitimate to wonder whether the loss of the opportunities for fame and fortune offered by the empire had something to do with the recent rise of Scottish nationalism.

January 1, 1975, 7:15 A.M.

By 1870, just when industrialization was gathering full force in Germany, Japan and the United States, Britain began to decline. A century of pioneering gave the British the feeling that there was little they had to learn from others. In the early decades of the Industrial Revolution Britain was receptive to technological innovations. After 1870 a new invention had to prove itself in other countries before it was accepted in Britain. The industrial decline was also due to the diversion of the energies of the British middle class into the aristocratic pastime of empire building.

The agitation about the population explosion is persuading many talented and enterprising Americans to have few children. The resulting change in the composition of the population will probably be not unlike that produced by war, which kills the strong and venturesome and increases the proportion of those least fit to improve and adorn mankind.

We see at present brilliant people agitate with all their might against the birth and advancement of brilliant Americans. They want to divert all wealth and energies toward the nurturing of the least endowed.

9:00 P.M.   I have spent a fortune this Christmas yet I do not feel impoverished. We shall celebrate every Christmas as if it were my last. The sky is the limit.

We spent the afternoon with Lili's family in Cupertino. The Fabilli women delight in singing together the songs they used to sing as children. The ninety-year-old mother joined in. It occurred to me that singing together could be a means of cultivating esprit de corps, of creating family ties among strangers. So would occasional common meals and opportunities for good conversation.

January 2, 9:10 A.M.

Through most of his existence man's survival depended on his ability to cope with nature. If the mind evolved as an aid in human survival it was primarily as an instrument for the mastery of nature. The mind is still at its best when tinkering with the mathematics that rule nature. It is awkward and often misleading when confronted with the task of comprehending and mastering man. Hence in a time like ours when man has become the main threat to human survival, intellectual faculties alone cannot solve our vital problems. Imagination, intuitive insights, and the lessons of experience are more critical than logic.

Revolutionaries are as a rule logicians, and when the dreams shaped by their logic come true they turn into nightmares. The harm done by self-appointed experts in human affairs is usually a product of a priori logic. Progressive experts in child-rearing assume logically that to raise independent adults children must be made self-reliant as early as possible. Events have proved, however, that children left to get in and out of trouble on their own feel abandoned. Where parents fail to exercise authority the peer group takes over, and members of a peer group are most conformist and least confident. Many young parents after the end of the Second World War, particularly the better educated and more affluent, were receptive to avant-garde ideas and followed the advice of know-all child-rearing experts who frowned on authority and exalted spontaneity. The 1960s saw the result: an adolescent counterculture of drift, drugs and appallingly conformist nonconformity.

January 3, 7:00 A.M.

If Russia sees a strong China as its greatest danger then a friendly, stable Europe at its back, willing to supply Russia with the products of its advanced technology, is more important than the propagation of Russian communism. A technologically inefficient communized Europe would be less useful than a friendly, efficient capitalist Europe. Moreover, there is no guarantee that some of the communized European countries might not sympathize with China.

The grotesqueness of Russia: It squats on a sixth of the world's surface yet does not allow its people to produce all the wheat, meat, vegetables and fruit they need. It has to buy food from capitalist countries. And what a grotesque spectacle it is to see one of the largest countries in the world—made large by despoiling its neighbors—pitting itself against tiny Israel and accusing it of imperialist expansion.

Russia does all it can to promote change in the non-communist world but is dead set against change inside its sphere of influence. America promotes change inside but fears change outside.

January 4, 9:00 A.M.
       Black and Chicano waitresses in cafeterias are usually niggardly with customers. Logic would expect them to be free with the white boss's substance and side with the poor customer. But it is not so. The reason is not that they are afraid of being reprimanded or fired. They simply do not love their customers. They probably also derive a sense of power from dishing out as little as possible. The most generous waitresses come from the Middle West. They love humanity and take plenty for granted.

6:30 P.M.   Most social thinkers of the nineteenth century were afraid that the entrance of the masses onto the stage of history would make democratic government impossible. Even the most liberal among the thinkers were obsessed with this fear. Bagehot, so insightful in other matters, thought that once the masses were given political power only education and prosperity could preserve social stability.

Bagehot's faith in the stabilizing effect of affluence and education must seem naïve to us who have seen how, during the 1960s, abundance and a multitude of semester intellectuals produced by the post-Sputnik education explosion brought this country to the brink of chaos.

It is puzzling that Disraeli should have known more about the nature of the masses than his liberal contemporaries. He sensed the conservatism and patriotism of common folk. It is perhaps true that a genuine conservative is more attuned to the eternal verities of human nature and of society. He is aware that the logic of events may draw from man's actions consequences which a priori logic cannot foresee. Disraeli's forebodings about England's future and his ideas on what keeps a nation vigorous and great have a poignant relevance at present. Must one be conservative or even reactionary if one wants to be thought up-to-date tomorrow?

January 5, 6:50 A.M.

I am both moved and irritated by Randolph Hearst's effort to justify himself in the eyes of his daughter Patty, despite her unspeakable behavior. He is not the kind of parent who can renounce his child. It reminds me of David and Absalom.

The nineteenth century was rich in new beginnings while the twentieth is a century of endings and harvests. Both the achievements and the crimes of the twentieth century are a harvest of what the nineteenth century sowed.

Guglielmo Ferrero, when describing the fabulous stability of the nineteenth century, says that "it could dream of anarchy, worship revolution, and amuse itself by destroying and reworking the world with its thought, while enjoying the most solid and perfect order that had ever been established on earth." The dreamers, schemers and thinkers were planting the seed of the apocalyptic events of the twentieth century.

As hard as breaking an ingrained habit is the discarding of a reform that is no longer relevant. Our time cries out for child labor—there are no children any more—but no one dares propose it.

January 6, 10:00 A.M.

The task of a United Germany should have been to enlarge Europe: to push Russia beyond the Urals, back into Asia. It was a fateful flaw of German statesmanship not to work for a wholehearted reconciliation with France and Britain at any price so as to be able to canalize all German energies eastward. It was also a flaw of French and British statesmanship not to encourage a German *Drang nach Osten*.

During the second quarter of the nineteenth century de Tocqueville, Jules Michelet and František Palacký knew that the role of a United Germany and of the Hapsburg empire was to serve as a buffer against Russia. But with the outburst of chauvinism after 1848 Europe's energies went into internal rivalries which culminated in the catastrophic civil war we know as the two World Wars.

One wonders whether a civilized, truly European Hitler might have rallied Europe in a grand undertaking to free western Russia of Stalinist slavery and tap the fabulous resources of the Eurasian land mass. Chances are that an envious France would have defeated such an attempt.

Someone said that the Russians are the only people who know how to be happy in prison. There is no reason why the present prison regime should not last indefinitely. Russia is big enough and rich enough to get along without an efficient utilization of its natural and human resources.

January 7, 8:15 A.M.

In both Britain and France intellectuals have been more affected by the loss of empire than businessmen, who were supposedly the chief beneficiaries of imperialism. It is true that many intellectuals denounced imperialism and called for its end, but when the empire was no more, life lost its spaciousness and grandeur.

Although Britain's loss of empire was more precipitate, it was not preceded by the defeat and humiliation experienced by the French during the Second World War. Hence the British intellectuals are weathering the crisis with grace and balance while the French need an exaggerated assertion of cultural superiority to sustain them through the ordeal of decline.

In both Britain and France intellectuals hug the illusion of a world constituency. "We have lost the empire but we have won a world audience." They curry favor with the intellectual elites in the decolonialized countries by making common cause with them against the white man. They cheer when white men are chased out of an African country or when the Occident's economy is laid low by exorbitant prices for oil and raw materials.

January 8, 6:50 A.M.

It is an outrage that with so much arable land Latin America and Russia should have to import grain. No one dares shame the representatives of these countries for their criminal interference with the productive capacity of their people. It is getting more and more difficult to see why this country should have any obligation toward the economically mismanaged parts of the world. It would be fitting if the American representative at the United Nations held up to public scorn the creators of hunger.

American farmers and manufacturers are easing Russia's domestic difficulties and make it possible for Russia to concentrate on armaments. Russia is gaining influence in the world not by giving foreign aid but by supplying military equipment and training. Communism is a failure as an economic system but may triumph as a military instrument.

January 9, 7:45 A.M.

What rankles Frenchmen is the decline of France relative to other European countries. France wants to be not a world power but the foremost European nation. If the present fuel debacle brings about a decline of Western Europe, France wants to make sure that it ends up sitting on top of the heap. To solve the fuel problem by force would result in a situation in which France could not play a paramount role. Hence France will urge submission to Arab dictates. It will also be for the abandonment of Israel and the cold-shouldering of the United States.

Finally, since the existence of an industrious, prosperous and stable West Germany automatically deflates all France-first rhetoric, one ought to expect French mischief to rekindle the hostility toward Germany. The rekindling will probably be the work not of government officials or businessmen but of the intellectual establishment.

It matters little who owns Britain's coal mines so long as the required tonnage is delivered at a reasonable price. If state- or union-owned mines will not deliver, the mines should be given to foreign workers, who will.

The fact that it matters little who owns the mines seems a breakthrough to a novel state of affairs.

Again and again I have the feeling that the British, beset by economic and political difficulties, have discovered something more prized than a sound economy, political stability, and even hope. Is it the good life? Visitors returning from crisis-ridden Britain tell how surprisingly pleasant and soothing life is in London.

January 10, 7:30 A.M.

The great cloth merchants of Florence and the great shipowners of Venice passionately loved their cities. They were

31

greedy for gold but they also strived to make their cities beautiful and famous. They saw it as their natural task to govern their cities and employed great artists and poets to commemorate their rule with immortal works. They saw it as their duty to spot and nurture talent and reward greatness.

In the Netherlands, too, the great cloth merchants and shipowners built a society in which wealth and power justified themselves by patronizing learning and the arts.

In America up to now the wealthy and powerful have shied away from personal involvement in the cultural life of their country. The foundations which bear their names are administered by intellectuals often not in sympathy with the ideals and goals of their capitalist benefactors. Yet the need for justifying the wealth and power of great corporations in the eyes of the people has never been greater. Why not hark back to Florence, Venice, Antwerp and Amsterdam? The great corporations could devote wealth and energies to cleaning up, improving and adorning our cities. Each large corporation might adopt a city and vie with other corporations to see whose city shines brightest. In the center of each financial district there should be a large plaza in which periodically poets, singers, storytellers and artists of every sort would compete for rich prizes. The corporations should see it as their duty to spot and encourage talent, and celebrate greatness. There should be social intimacy between the powerful and the creative.

January 11, 6:30 A.M.

In the eighteenth century the educated minorities had much in common in all European countries, and even in Russia. The differentiation of national characteristics came in the nineteenth century. Reading about eighteenth-century Englishmen one is startled how Dostoevskian some of them were. Russia remained stuck in the eighteenth century.

The crisis of our time stems from the fact that social institutions have become as vulnerable as individuals. The attributes which made institutions less subject to the vicissitudes of chance and circumstances have lost much of their effectiveness. Traditions and axioms no longer find unquestioned acceptance.

I wonder whether the fences and taboos which used to surround institutions, and the savage sanctions against anyone who laid hands on them, originated in an awareness of their vulnerability. We have seen how a scratch on an institution easily develops into a cancer.

America will become common—will lose its uniqueness—when it ceases to be the fatherland of common people.

The Soviet Union has neither soviets nor unions.

It needs a despot not only to turn free men into slaves but slaves into free men.

January 12, 1:00 P.M.
      There is a leveling process going on at present all over the globe. There are now rich backward countries dictating to poor advanced countries. The revulsion from work is bringing capitalist economies down to the communist level. Freedom no longer energizes people and no longer creates plenty. One wonders whether, once the leveling process has run its course, freedom will still matter. Will people continue to run from non-free to free countries?

It is uncanny how when trying to make sense of what has happened to America since 1960 we find the nearest analogies in Weimar Germany, pre-revolutionary Russia, and Britain in the early decades of the industrial revolution. America is becoming not so much like other countries as like other countries' pasts.

In a preceding entry on the flow of influence (Dec. 27) I should have pointed out that influence flows from high points

33

of the human landscape to the low (that it follows a hydraulic model) only in the rare cases when one segment of mankind executes a leap that changes the quality of history. The domestication of plants and animals in the Fertile Crescent was such a leap, and so were the founding of the earliest cities in Sumer and the coming of the industrial revolution in the Occident.

January 13, 9:30 A.M.

I am reading a book on Hegel by Professor Walter Kaufman. After 154 pages I still have not an inkling of what Hegel was after. The time he lived in (1770–1831) was as eventful and unsettled as our own. No one knew what the next morning would bring. Yet here were a number of German professors, living practically on the battlefield (Jena), who were totally absorbed in producing thousands of pages of abstruse philosophy, convinced that they alone had a hold on the ultimate truth. They were drunk with words.

Hegel wrote his *Phenomenology of the Mind* in an incredibly short time—in the time it would take to transcribe the manuscript. He finished the book during the battle of Jena. Starting for the publisher in the morning he was surprised to see the streets of Jena full of French soldiers. Here is what Professor Kaufman has to say about the book. "The whole style of the *Phenomenology* is such that students and scholars are almost bound to ask themselves: What is the man talking about? Whom does he have in mind? Indeed—and this is crucial—the obscurity and whole manner are such that these questions are almost bound to replace the question whether what Hegel says is right."

It never ceases to amaze me that for over a century brilliant people derived a sense of chosenness from their ability to understand Hegel's *Phenomenology.*

I said that the time Hegel lived in was like our own. Actually there was a vital difference. The people who lived through the French Revolution and its Napoleonic aftermath were full of hope and illusions. They felt they were at the birth of a new world far superior to anything that had been in the past. We have the feeling that we are living in an absurd century with a dark age waiting for us at the end.

January 14, 6:30 A.M.

Americans have often been accused by Europeans of confusing quality with quantity. Yet this has been the sin of European philosophers, particularly the Germans. The main idea is to produce a thick book.

Ballet dancers are the only creative people who accept retirement as natural. It occurs to me that if thinking is a ballet of ideas, the thinking mind too should accept the fact that age makes dancing difficult.

To God eternity is as a day while to a one-day fly a day is an eternity. Our time is getting near to that of a one-day fly. A year now is as a century. We measure eras not in centuries nor even in decades. Every five years or so we have a new era. We have two or three turning points in a decade.

An individual alone in the world can feel guilty but not ashamed. Shame is a social manifestation, and the more compact the society the more intense the sense of shame. This brings us up against a paradox: monolithic Russia is the most shameless society the world has seen. Everybody betrays, everybody lies, everybody confesses—no one feels shame. Russians may feel guilty but not ashamed. It is legitimate to wonder, therefore, whether Russia with all its totalitarian compactness constitutes a genuine society. Mihaylo Mihaylov maintains "there is no society at all in communist countries." And since shame is uniquely human—Aristotle defined man as "the beast with red cheeks"—the lack of shame in communist countries is a symptom of dehumanization.

January 15, 6:40 A.M.

The fact that there is no such a thing as happiness does not mean that there is no unhappiness.

Young Americans are begging in the streets of cities all over the world. They are feared as shoplifters and suspected of drug smuggling. Will we ever recover from the disastrous 1960s?

No two successive centuries have been so unlike each other as the nineteenth and the twentieth. The nineteenth century was stable, rational, hopeful and free. The twentieth century has been hectic, soaked with the blood of innocents, fearful of the future, crisscrossed with frontiers that impede free movement, irrational and absurd.

Some of the disastrous absurdities of the twentieth century: the First World War, the Russian Revolution, the Versailles Peace Treaty, Prohibition, the Great Depression, the Roosevelt administration (which tried to end the Depression by killing pigs and dumping wheat), the Hitler revolution, the Second World War, the 1960s.

January 16, 6:00 A.M.

The taste and capacity for prophesying are fueled by a dislike of the present and a sense of homelessness. The ancient Hebrews who squatted on the highway of history and were trampled by marching and countermarching armies became a prophetic nation par excellence. The Russians suspended between East and West and at home in neither produced a remarkable number of prophetic individuals during the nineteenth century. On the other hand, the English though immersed in the Old Testament were not given to prophesying. Never before have there been people who felt so wholly at home in the world as did nineteenth-century Englishmen. They felt at home wherever they went—the whole world was their backyard.

4:45 P.M.   The idea about the non-prophetic Englishmen does not stand up. Think of the prophetic temperaments of Disraeli and Carlyle. It is true that Disraeli was an un-English Englishman and Carlyle a passionate Scotsman. But to H. G. Wells and Arnold Toynbee prophesying was as natural as breathing. There were probably many others.

January 17, 10:20 A.M.
The generation that plunged into the First World War was up to its neck in axioms. It took civilization, progress, monetary stability, freedom, order, rationality for granted. There were, it is true, intellectuals who lusted to tear down all that existed and create a perfect world. But they too had a belief in the lastingness of things. They did not expect their words to become flesh. The war saw the wholesale slaughter of axioms.

Actually, the slaughter of axioms was as much the work of the Russian Revolution as of the war. Indeed, the revolution marked a sharper break with the past than did the war. Despite the frightful bloodshed, the First World War remained within a civilized framework. The treatment of prisoners and of civilians followed international agreements. To Lenin, all civilized usages were bourgeois tricks. He made a mockery of honor, truth, freedom and democracy.

Had there been no Lenin there would have been no Hitler.

In 1848 the Czech historian Palacký, in a letter to the German parliament in Frankfurt, urged the bolstering of the Hapsburg empire as a bulwark against a Russia that "expands of itself decade after decade." He saw Russia as "an infinite and inexplicable evil, a misfortune without measure and bound."

Later, when chauvinism blurred the concept of Europe, Palacký, caught in the confrontation between German and Slav, changed his tune and became pro-Russian.

January 18, 7:00 A.M.

It gives me pleasure that at my age I am so ready to learn all I can from Steven and Eric. I shall probably learn more from my dealings with Eric than from any experience I ever had. Up to now I have always consulted my own needs first. Having lived by myself most of my life, I have not been compelled by circumstances to live myself into other people's difficulties. I have been generous with money but I have not been truly compassionate.

We are flying today to Santa Barbara. I am all packed, waiting for Lili. The plane leaves at nine but we are going to have a leisurely breakfast at the airport. The talk about the Bible* weighs on my mind.

It remains incredible that hardly anyone had an inkling of what the First World War was going to be. Not only were practical people—businessmen and soldiers—totally unaware but writers, artists, scholars and scientists were without premonitions of impending catastrophe. Stefan Zweig described the mood on the eve of the war: "I never loved that old earth more than in those last years before the First World War, never hoped more ardently for European unity, never had more faith in the future than then."

The apocalyptic catastrophe of the First World War came after a century of stability, peace and hope. Nowadays a child knows more about the reality of the human condition than wise men knew in pre-1914 Europe. You read of "the hectic air of festivity and the gay expectancy" with which Europe entered the war. "Soldiers were pelted with flowers, cheering crowds on the sidewalks, ladies in light summer dresses on

_____
*At the University of California at Santa Barbara.

the balconies." Never again will men march to war the way they did in 1914.

January 19, 2:30 P.M.

We are back in San Francisco. After my speech a good-looking young couple came over to talk with me. The young man spoke haltingly of the decay of so many old people in retirement; their minds become feeble and so on. He asked what it was that kept me going in my seventies. I answered that as long as an old man keeps learning, particularly if he can learn from his grandchildren, his mind is not likely to fall apart. It also helps a lot if, by the grace of God, he has people he loves and who love him. Still the fact remains that everybody declines in old age.

America has never ceased to be an experiment. In every generation America has still to prove that a society founded on values cherished by common people can endure, and that it is possible to fuse hordes of heterogeneous immigrants into one nation indivisible.

The attitude toward theory: Late in the eighteenth century there were many who thought theory more potent than action, that in the words of Hegel: "Once the realm of notion is revolutionized, actuality does not hold out." Heine predicted that the words piled up by German philosophers would eventually bring about a revolution compared with which all other revolutions would seem a storm in a teacup.

The men of action who initiated the industrial revolution made light of theory. They discovered how things worked by trial and error, and had faith in feel and know-how. However, the atomic bomb and Sputnik have made theory supreme. The practical lowbrows who made fun of theory as a species of wind now see it as a mighty explosive that may blow up the universe. Has this awe of theory undermined capitalist confidence?

39

January 20, 6:30 A.M.

I have just come across a remarkable prediction made by Matthew Arnold almost a hundred years ago: "I have a conviction that there is a real and almost imminent danger of England losing immeasurably in all ways, declining into a sort of greater Holland, for want of ideas, for want of perceiving how the world is going and must go, and preparing herself accordingly. The conviction haunts me. . . . I would rather not live to see the change come to pass, for we shall all deteriorate under it."

I must get hold of a biography of Sir Edward Grey, another prophetic Englishman. He recognized from the beginning the catastrophic dimensions and consequences of the First World War.

January 21, 6:40 A.M.

Of late I have been losing my way in my dreams. Suddenly I do not know where I am. Dreaming with me is not an escape from an untenable existence. Sometimes when I lie down to sleep, I am overcome by weariness at the thought of what's ahead of me.

I have always felt that the people I love could easily renounce me. How often have I felt that the connection had been cut and that I was a stranger, alone in the world. Yet how often too has my heart glowed with the knowledge that I am unconditionally and unalterably loved and cherished.

The best education will not immunize a person against corruption by power. The best education does not automatically make people compassionate. We know this more clearly than any preceding generation. Our time has seen the best-educated society, situated in the heart of the most civilized part of the world, give birth to the most murderously vengeful government in history.

Forty years ago the philosopher Alfred North Whitehead

thought it self-evident that you would get a good government if you took power out of the hands of the acquisitive and gave it to the learned and the cultivated. At present, a child in kindergarten knows better than that.

It is remarkable how many outstanding persons who achieved much in life were savagely asinine at the age of twenty. "What They Said at Twenty" would make a curious collection. I just read a statement made by Dos Passos in 1916 when he was twenty: "My only hope is in revolution—in the wholesale assassination of all statesmen, capitalists, warmongers, jingoists, inventors, scientists."

January 22, 8:00 A.M.

An individual can probably thrive without illusions, but it is doubtful whether a wholly disillusioned society can be vigorous. Such a society will be awkward in dealing with internal adversaries and will not know how to impose its values on the new generation and on outsiders. The thirty million immigrants who came to America after the Civil War were smoothly assimilated by a society that had extravagant illusions about the future. On the other hand, the present integration of twenty some million Negroes is proceeding in a climate of disillusionment.

In the past I could carry a complex train of thought in my head, formulating and revising, without writing down a word until I had it all tied up. At present I cannot think without pen in hand. Clearly, old age has its own requirements and rules. The old must break with the past and learn anew.

To function well, the old need deference and special treatment. In societies that revere age, the old look beautiful.

Old age is not a rumor.

The things which corrupt the young may help the old stay young.

January 23, 7:15 A.M.

I am reading Trevelyan's biography of Sir Edward Grey. On the evening before war was declared, as he looked through the window of his room in the Foreign Office and saw the lamps being lit in the summer dusk, Sir Edward said to a friend: "The lamps are going out all over Europe; we shall not see them lit again in our lifetime." Next day, in a note, he expressed his dismay: "Europe is in the most terrible trouble it has ever known in civilized times, and no one can say what will be left at the end."

Grey's passion was for bird watching, fly fishing, and hiking. But his darkened spirits enabled him to sense the fate awaiting the Occident. In a letter in 1913 he foresaw a disastrous end for industrial civilization: "This boasted civilization that has defiled beautiful country, made hideous cities, been built up and maintained by ghastly competition and pressure, makes men swarm together and multiply horribly, is so abominable that God will sweep it away."

January 24, 6:30 A.M.

Everyone expects 1975 to be a year of decision for the Occident. My fear is that it will be a year of protracted crisis. It is the lingering crisis that debilitates. An explosion would cleanse the air. I would welcome a blowing up of the oil wells in the Persian Gulf. A dramatic end of the fossil-fuel age could be the opening act in the renewal and rebirth of the Occident. The balance of the century should be devoted to the search for cheaper and cleaner fuels. In the meantime the Occident should adopt a simpler and slower mode of life and use its manpower in a concerted effort to cleanse air and water of pollution, replenish the soil, reforest the hills, and clean up the cities. The added bonus of such an undertaking would be to give our vast population of adolescents a healthy way of attaining manhood and probably accelerate racial integration.

Who in the 1950s had a premonition of the witches' sabbath that would be enacted in the 1960s? Once events have taken place, a horde of learned commentators demonstrate that the unexpected was inevitable. Actually, chance, stupidity and cowardice were chief factors. Nothing was inevitable.

6:45 P.M.   I walked along the waterfront for about three hours. It has been a long time since I was there. The walk is easy since there are many places where I can sit down and ease my right leg. I hardly saw a familiar face. Almost all the people I worked with have retired. It was a surprise to be recognized and greeted by young longshoremen who came to the waterfront after my retirement. Several of them are the sons of longshoremen.

January 25, 8:15 A.M.
Were it not for women and children the industrial revolution might not have got started. They were made to work twelve hours a day, seven days a week, from the word go. Adult males stubbornly refused to be harnessed to this endless grind. The masters were unbelievably ruthless and arrogant. We read that in 1830 there were still forty-two traditional holidays. Some years later there were only four. The middle class that started the industrial revolution lived in its own world and cared less for the people who worked in the factories than for beasts of burden. The lower orders were seen as a different species.

The working people of Britain began the industrial revolution with a whimper and they are now bringing it to an end with a bang. They now have the upper hand. But the reversal of roles is taking place in a Britain impoverished and dispirited.

The English used to make good masters and good servants. Since they lost their Empire, the English are no longer masters and have ceased to be good servants.

43

A generation that wearies of technology is bound to turn to magic. Those who refuse to use machines that move mountains will pray for a faith that moves mountains.

To give equality to people who cannot be equal is to intensify their feeling of inequality. So too to give freedom to people who cannot help themselves is to increase their feeling of oppression. Moreover, to give freedom and equality to people who cannot help themselves is to rob them of soul-soothing alibis.

January 26, 5:00 A.M.
　　　　Old age has made me common. I have the typical aches and predicaments of the old. It is true that my nose is not dripping when my head nods in drowsiness and I manage to keep the corners of my mouth clean.

It is good to remind myself that it is by sheer wild luck that I have in my old age enough to live on and no money worries at all. So far I have had no misfortunes, and at seventy-three I feel that I have won the race. It is true that I am easy on myself. I have a right to an unstrenuous old age. But it must be free of boredom and a feeling of stagnation. This means that I must go on thinking, learning and writing. All I can allow myself is a slower tempo.

January 27, 8:30 A.M.
　　　　Nations tend to see their great men as the expression of their quintessence and uniqueness. Great men are also assumed to embody the spirit of their age. Actually, the essential characteristic of a great man is his timelessness and universality. The great man of any age is our contemporary.

It is by their commonness that people are linked to their time. Hence, by how much a great man is of his age by so much is he less great.

Did anyone in the 1930s see clearly the kinship between communists and Nazis? The tendency has been to see Nazism as a poisonous by-product of decaying capitalism. Actually, as I have suggested, there could not have been a Hitler without a Lenin.

One could, of course, argue that Lenin himself was a product of declining capitalism. A non-enfeebled capitalist society would have wrung the necks of potential Lenins.

What needs explaining is the source of Stalin's unchallenged dominance over the Russians. There were no conspiracies against Stalin at any time. The question is whether without Stalin's pathological suspicion of conspiracies there would have been such a total absence of conspiracies.

Russia's refusal to let her Jews go should have given rise to the most scathing anti-Russian propaganda. The words *Russia* and *prison* should have been made synonymous. The trouble is that we no longer derive joy from making Russia look ridiculous.

January 28, 6:45 A.M.
Last night I heard young people declaim about lonesomeness in America. They thought that the lack of warm communal life is dehumanizing. The hunger for communal life is characteristic of the young and probably has a sexual nexus. Under normal conditions there is a healthy mixture of aloneness and togetherness. Eating, drinking and talking with friends after a day's work makes life glorious. But to be wholly immersed in communal life is sick. Despite the widespread hunger for communality, this country has not been a good milieu for communes. America was pioneered mostly by loners and it is still ideal for people who want to be left alone.

The birth of the nineteenth century: the prelude to this most stable and peaceful century was a massive hemorrhage, a twenty-year war. We cannot blame war for the demented savagery of the twentieth century. It is legitimate to wonder whether the nineteenth century would have become what it was had the French come out of the Napoleonic wars as conquerors. The reason the First World War did not wind up the way other wars (including the Second World War) did was that France wanted to be the foremost nation in Europe and would not leave Germany alone.

January 29, 7:00 A.M.
　　　　Do eras vary in their degree of forgetfulness? Certainly our century forgets more readily than any preceding era. It is difficult in the 1970s to remember the 1950s. So much has happened!

The tendency to forget does not originate in the need to efface unpleasant memories. Germany could not forget its humiliation after the First World War and France its humiliation during the Second World War. Forgetfulness is linked with a break in continuity. The total difference between the 1960s and the 1950s created a feeling of remoteness. The same is true of the sharp break between the 1960s and 70s.

There is a tendency to turn insoluble problems into taboos that must not be mentioned. In this country the racial problem is kept out of conversation. In Britain, the revulsion from work which is the main cause of the present crisis is hardly ever mentioned.

We somehow take it for granted that drastic changes undermine authority. In the new book I have a short chapter on change and authority in which I show that the most successful drastic changes took place in an authoritarian atmosphere. A society racked by drastic change needs a strong framework of authority and an anchor of continuity to keep it from falling apart. Yet the intellectual establishment which advocates the

46

permissive society thinks that the new can germinate and grow only when it breaks through the integuments of authority.

January 30, 9:50 A.M.

After all the battles, all the triumphs, all the suffering, and all the glory Britain has become a small island inhabited by tired people who want to pass their days with as little toil and worry as possible.

Right now, hope has become the monopoly of the slavemasters in Russia. In the free world, desire has taken the place of hope and it looks as if soon the Occident will weary of desire.

We can learn more from the present than from all of history. The belly of the world has been ripped open and we can see with our own eyes things which past generations could only guess at. There should be a new type of historian who will mine the present for clues about the past.

In a free society it is necessary to spell out what people cannot do, while in an authoritarian society it is vital to spell out what people can do.

An America that in the decades before the First World War assimilated thirty million immigrants had no difficulty transmitting its values to the young. It was an America that had hope, confidence and nerve—the nerve to demand much from its children and from the arriving immigrants.

January 31, 7:10 A.M.

No one has explained the present failure of nerve of people in authority. The erosion of authority in government, family, school, factory and even in the armed forces is the most bothersome phenomenon of our time. Many blame it on change: rapid, drastic change disintegrates values, renders skills and experience obsolete, and drains adults of confidence. Others see the cause in affluence. Well, affluence is no more. We also know that the most drastic changes of the past—the modernization of Japan and the rapid industrialization of Germany—were realized in authoritarian societies. There was no erosion of authority during England's rapid transformation in the early decades of the industrial revolution. So too in this country, the rapid changes after the Civil War occurred in an atmosphere of political and cultural conservatism.

My hunch is that the reason drastic change erodes authority at present is that we are without hope. Where things have not changed, authority remains intact even in the absence of hope. But when the social pot is boiling with change and no one knows what is cooking authority seems helpless and loses its power to awe.

February 1, 6:40 A.M.

I wonder what would happen if next year, on America's two hundredth birthday, an American President proclaimed a year of total migration, of the free movement of people all over the planet. Travel on trains, ships and planes would be free. Everyone would have a chance to find the country he loved best. Would the consequences be catastrophic? America might get at least thirty million new immigrants to love and cherish it. It is also possible that many adversary intellectuals might be too shy to rush back to a country they ridiculed as a pig's heaven.

When one sees the present rush of Jews to get out of Russia, it is startling to remember how blindly German Jews clung to Germany after Hitler's takeover, and even after the passage of the Nuremberg laws in 1935. When in 1938 life became unbearable and they were finally willing to leave, it was too late—the outside world slammed its doors against Jewish refugees.

7:00 P.M.   We drove to Salinas to see a friend who is in the hospital. She had a bad car accident which left her paralyzed from the hip down. She is beginning to recover. Her spinal cord is smashed but the nerves are not severed. She has extraordinary vitality. It frightens me to think how our lives are more than ever dominated by accidents—the cruel deities.

On the way back we stopped for a cup of coffee in the small town of Gilroy. Prices were low, service excellent, the place spotless. The faces of the women serving us—all middle-aged— were fresh and good to look at. For a moment it seemed to me senseless that I should live in San Francisco.

February 2, 7:20 A.M.

I have not found the reason why a society without illusions becomes flabby and unsure of itself. De Tocqueville has it that "Everything is feared when nothing is ardently desired." There is also the Spanish proverb: "Whoever is not called upon to struggle is forgotten by God."

How vital is experience to the creative flow? A creative person is not eaten up by his experience. Indeed, it is remarkable how the genuinely creative instinctively shy away from a full-blooded experience. They want to make much out of very little, and need but a crumb to know the taste of a loaf.

America's readiness to share its bounty with millions of European immigrants has been singularly wise though the motives which prompted the policy were not mainly altruistic. Had South Africa, Rhodesia or even Canada embraced a policy of unrestricted immigration its survival would be more unquestioned than it is now.

When we speak of authority at present we usually have in mind governmental authority. Actually, social order is most

49

firm when imposed and maintained by the limited authorities of family, school, church, job, neighborhood and so on. In 1848 the Spaniard Donoso-Cortés predicted that "when religious discipline ceases to exist there cannot be enough of government; all despotisms will not be sufficient." This holds true to some extent of the other minor authorities.

6:00 P.M. Walked leisurely through the park. Wound up at Tommy's Joynt at five and ate lustily a heap of fettuccini topped with beef burgundy. The only idea that occurred to me was that the First World War was a dividing line for emigration from Europe. The stability of nineteenth-century Europe was in no small part due to the emigration of the restless and disaffected. Had America and the British Empire welcomed emigrants from Europe after the First World War, there might have been neither a Fascist nor a Nazi revolution.

February 3, 9:30 A.M.
    I have come across several articles by the American playwright Arthur Miller in which he sets out to denounce Stalin's purges and Brezhnev's invasion of Czechoslovakia but ends up denouncing America.
    Living in America, Arthur Miller wrote all the plays he wanted to write, had them produced, and was amply rewarded by money and fame. He also managed to have everything his heart desired, including the most fabulous blonde of his day. Why then this loathing of America? The only explanation I can think of is that Miller is too self-righteous and self-important to admit the gross stupidity of his Stalinist commitment. He must go on trying to convince the world that there is not much to choose between Russia and America.

Despite the drastic changes all around us, it is remarkable how rare is the sense of newness. Perhaps to feel that something is truly new we have first to expect it. It is the realization of the expected that strikes us as the birth of the new.

I am haunted by Tennyson's lament in old age: "I am the greatest master of English that ever lived and I have nothing to say." He intoxicated himself by endlessly repeating his name.

February 4, 5:50 A.M.
It seems hardly credible that this country should have attempted Prohibition. What confidence, and what ignorance! It certainly is a different country now. Both Prohibition and the Great Depression had profound effects on our national character. In any discussion of the breakdown of authority in this country the "noble experiment" should be given a prominent place.

The communists try to eliminate the subtly interwoven appetites, inclinations and impulses which normally keep people striving and searching. They want a society that is energized by noble motives untainted by gross promptings. It is like trying to eliminate sexual desire as a factor in procreation.

Now and then it seems to me that we have Russia over a barrel. She is stuck with an economic system she cannot make work. Only superior people like the Chinese and the Jews (kibbutzim) can make communism work. The Russians also have nine hundred million Chinese breathing down their necks. We must never try to induce Russia to abandon communism, and we must do all we can to encourage her to invade China and see to it that she gets bogged down there for good.

February 5, 7:00 A.M.
The warrior tribes of Europe felt uncomfortable with Christianity. Their fervent belief was shot through with resent-

ment. How much of this unarticulated resentment leaked out as hatred of the Jews? Both God and Jesus were Jewish.

Many outstanding men had outstanding mothers. An outstanding father seems to handicap his children. I ought to say "his sons," for it may well be that women are not handicapped by strong fathers.

Nowadays, anyone who dwells on the difficult problems which confront a society is considered reactionary. Many liberals are hostile toward any evidence that there are problems that cannot be solved or that the results of reforms are often the opposite of what the reformers intended.

It was only in the late 1840s that adult Englishmen finally became steady workers. Someone clever suggested that when the children who made the industrial revolution possible (January 25) grew up they became steady adult workers. Today I found the following in Arthur Bryant's *English Saga:* "Many of the child workers were crippled for life; few grew to mature manhood or womanhood. . . . Every street had its company of cripples, of permanently aged and arthritic youths bent double and limping."

February 6, 6:35 A.M.
        Walter Laqueur in *Out of the Ruins of Europe* wonders why for so many young Americans and some of their elders America has become "the epitome of repression, a country unfit to live in." It is leprous vanity that does it: pretentious nonentities wanting to avenge themselves for being ignored, for not being given power. It is these inflated zeros who denounce anyone who speaks well of America as, at least, an ethnocentrist.

The phenomenal conformity in America is perhaps an indication of how lost people feel on this vast continent. As Whitehead suggested, when a man is lost his chief question is not where he is but where the others are.

It is also true that in a competitive society to act and be like others is a guarantee of not being left behind. My hunch is that competitive people feel alone in the world.

Somehow connected with the fact that creative periods are relatively brief is the fact that outstanding achievements do not emerge slowly but appear full-blown. The reason is probably that anything perfect is the creation of an individual and evolves in less than the span of an individual life.

I wonder whether a vigorous mass organization is at all possible without a chauvinist appeal. A socialist movement must become nationalist to gain a hold over the masses. There is treason of intellectuals but never of the masses.

Febrary 7, 6:45 A.M.
        Where Christianity was fighting for its life against Islam, Church and State became one. The result was something like a Christian caliphate. This happened in Spain, Byzantium and Russia; and these countries, like Islam, became culturally and economically stagnant. Only in European countries away from the embattled borders did the division between Church and State make possible the birth of individual freedom and the dynamism of stretched souls.

This country was in worse shape in the 1930s than it is today. There was more unemployment, there was hunger, and there was a greater paralysis of will. Capitalism was more bankrupt and discredited than it is in the 1970s. Yet the feeling of doom is stronger now. There is a widespread feeling that our economic system and our civilization are nearing their end. In the 1930s we still had values, ideals, hopes, illusions, certitudes. In the 1970s many people see life drained of meaning, and there is hardly a certitude left. Arthur Koestler compares the impact of the 1960s on our traditional values to the impact the European invaders had on the traditional life of the American Indian and the Pacific Islanders. The 1960s were decisive. We cannot understand what is happening in the 1970s unless we know what happened in the 1960s.

February 8, 10:10 A.M.

Vienna at the turn of the century was passionately preoccupied with doom. I can never understand how a band of highly educated people can, in normal times, become obsessed with the contemplation of apocalyptic dénouements. It is hard to realize that there are persons so convinced of their superiority and fitness to rule the world that they lust for an end of all that exists in order to get their chance.

It seems strange that a pathological lust for power should be more often a characteristic of cultured men of words than of lowbrow soldiers, industrialists and the like.

Old age is teaching me to take joy in the existence of beautiful and desirable things without wanting to possess or even savor them. I have not enjoyed the sight of beautiful women in the past as I do now. The same is true of the new magnificent buildings, paved plazas, fountains and flower beds. Life seems richer now.

February 9, 6:15 A.M.

Oil from the floor of the North Sea will not automatically end Britain's economic crisis. British workers are not likely to exert themselves and become efficient in the foreseeable future. To solve its labor problem an oil-rich Britain may have to retire British workers at forty or less and bring in foreign workers. The Renaissance was the age of mercenary soldiers, ours is an age of mercenary labor.

The present inability of parents to pass on their values to their children may be partly due to the fact that most teachers, particularly in the big cities, do not share the values of run-of-the-mill parents. Indeed, many teachers see it as their duty to imbue students with values diametrically opposed to those of their parents—to prepare students for the "new reality."

February 10, 7:10 A.M.

What were the terrible 1960s (February 7) and where did they come from?

To begin with, the 1960s did not start in 1960. They started in 1957. A bell rings in my mind every time I hear the date 1957 mentioned. On October 4, 1957, the Russians placed a medicine-ball-sized satellite in orbit. It needs an effort to remember how stunned we were when we discovered that the clodhopping Russians were technologically ahead of us, and that we would have to catch up with them. We reacted hysterically. We set out to produce scientists and technologists wholesale by shoveling billions into the universities. And where the billions went there went also millions of persons who were not primarily interested in learning but wanted a piece of the action.

Thus Khrushchev's Sputnik toy brought about a change in the tilt of America's social landscape from the marketplace to the universities. After October 1957, many young people who would normally have gone into business ended up climbing academic ladders and throwing their weight around in literary and artistic cliques from Manhattan to Berkeley, California.

It was to be expected that the potential business tycoons would feel ill at ease on the campus. Where was the action? The university seemed to them a bloated, sluggish giant cut off from the stream of life. They were going to wake up the academic world and turn the university into an instrument of power. They were going to make history, which is an acceptable substitute for making and losing millions. It was these misplaced tycoons who set the tone and shaped events in the 1960s.

February 11, 9:30 A.M.

It is of interest that almost exactly a hundred years before Sputnik this country experienced another change in the tilt of its social landscape, but in the opposite direction—from the academy to the marketplace.

The first half of the nineteenth century was the age of the gentry, whose preoccupation was with education, cultural affairs and public service. But the opening of the West in the 1850s caught the imagination of the young, and the sons of the gentry scattered in all directions. Many who would have become teachers, ministers, writers or artists were seeking their fortunes in railroads, mining, manufacturing and the like. Instead of potential business tycoons throwing their weight around on campuses, as we had in the 1960s, there were potential poets and philosophers washed into business careers. I have always felt that it was not conventional businessmen but misplaced poets and philosophers who gave American business its Promethean sweep and drive. To a potential philosopher turned businessman all action is of one kind. He combines mines, railroads, oil fields, factories the way a philosopher collates and generalizes ideas.

9:00 P.M.   How strange that misplaced philosophers should have become grandiose builders while misplaced men of action became revolutionary wreckers. It is probably true as I suggested long ago in *The True Believer* that revolutionary intellectuals are mostly people "whose talents and temperament equip them ideally for a life of action but are condemned by circumstances to rust away in idleness." Most of the outstanding revolutionary leaders of our time spent the best part of their lives talking their heads off in cafés and meetings.

The significant fact is that men of action metamorphosed into men of words are more readily corrupted by power than conventional men of action. Words are a potent source of self-righteousness; they serve to mask questionable motives, and justify ruthlessness. Paradoxically, the metamorphosed man of action has faith in the magical powers of words. He becomes irrational and primitive and is a threat to civilized life. Though we find it hard to accept that "In the beginning was the Word," and that words created the world, we know that words can ignite genocidal passions and squash civilized societies. It is not hard for us to believe that words may eventually destroy our world.

February 12, 6:45 A.M.

Some of the potential business tycoons washed by Sputnik into academic careers became truly creative. They became outstanding sociologists, philosophers, scientists, even Nobel Prize winners. Still, there was something that distinguished them from regular scholars. They did not see learning as an end in itself. They saw words, ideas and theories as instruments of momentous action and history making as a vital component of an intellectual existence. They felt superior to the trivial businessmen and politicians who were running the country. They were going to create a new society in which every act was pregnant with meaning and destiny hovered over everyday life.

It is interesting that whereas the potential philosophers who became businessmen were uniquely American, unlike businessmen anywhere else, the potential tycoons who became academics were like intellectuals everywhere. They were twin brothers of intellectuals in Latin America, Europe, Asia and even in Africa.

In a previous entry (January 2) I described the effects of permissive child rearing promoted by avant-garde experts after the Second World War. It is clear that where parents abdicate authority the peer group takes over, and members of a peer group are utterly conformist. In 1964 a considerable segment of the student population was made up of eighteen-year-olds who were born in 1946 and were the products of a permissive upbringing. They were putty in the hands of any two-bit manipulator.

I happened to be in Berkeley in 1964 when the first wave of the new generation hit the campus of the University of California. President Clark Kerr made me a professor. It was my first taste of getting paid for doing nothing. They gave me a room on the eighth floor of Barrows Hall, where I held open house one afternoon a week. So I was right in the midst of the mess when the Free Speech Movement exploded in 1964.

The spark which set off the explosion was the discovery made by the students that the power structure of the university was manned by toothless lions. President Clark Kerr, one of the finest products of our culture, knew how to build a great university but did not know how to defend it. He had not an inkling of the vulnerability of institutions—that they are more vulnerable than individuals—and did not know the first thing about the nature of authority. I cannot resist the feeling that things might have turned out differently had President Kerr had a taste for theorizing. He might have known that authority is an instrument for the repression of individual willfulness and that social authority had its origin in the need to tame juveniles as they came out from underneath parental authority. Instead, President Kerr dealt with the rampaging juveniles as if they were his equals, and a punk like Mario Savio, the leader of the Free Speech Movement, ran circles around the great Clark Kerr. Much of the teaching at the University of California was done by teaching assistants not much older than the students. Monkeys with academic degrees opened all the cages and let the tigers out into the street.

I remember how one afternoon, as I stood on the eighth-floor balcony of Barrows Hall and watched swinish punks lay low the proud institution of the University of California, there flashed before my mind's eye an event of long ago. On the evening of November 16, 1532, the swineherd Francisco Pizarro pulled down the Inca Atahualpa from his proud litter and in scarcely three hours the most powerful state of pre-Columbian America was broken forever.

The people who want, and are fit, to live in a free society cultivate patience, and make of compromise a holy cause. The militants who clamor for freedom most of the time want power—power to retaliate. The means for establishing freedom are altogether different from the means of attaining power.

To William James the most crucial habit of an effective democracy is "a fierce and merciless resentment towards every man or set of men who break the public peace." How strange these words must sound in the ears of present-day militants!

February 13, 8:00 A.M.

 Psychoanalysts have a bias for deep, obscure causes. It was to be expected that the psychoanalyst Franz Alexander *(Western Mind in Transition)* should find that "a spiritual change preceded the First World War"; that the war only gave the coup de grâce to a spent cultural and political structure. He maintains that "the signs of decline presaging apocalypse were numerous and steadily growing." The main sign was a shift from a search for absolutes to an acceptance of relativity in all human endeavors. He sees an interconnection between Einsteinian physics, the new interpretation of space in cubistic painting, cultural relativism in anthropology, the war, the departure from the gold standard, and the rejection of classical rules of diplomacy. It was this pernicious relativism that prevented Europe from regaining its equilibrium when the war was over.

Actually, we have the testimony of knowledgeable observers on the stability and hopefulness of the pre-war era. To Alfred North Whitehead, who was immersed in the new physics, the period 1880–1910 was "one of the happiest times that I know of in the history of mankind. . . . We often used to speak of what a wonderful world to live in our children would have." The inability to pick things up after the war was due largely to France's determination to prevent Germany's recovery as a great power, and Lenin's rejection of civilized values as bourgeois prejudices.

February 14, 7:45 A.M.

When I think of what I have missed most of my life, I also think of all that I have been spared.

There are many books I have not read. I have never laid eyes on *Das Kapital* or the *Interpretation of Dreams*. I know of course more or less what the books are about, but something has kept me from getting into them.

I scorned Marx without having read him. Marx never did a day's work in his life, and knew as much about the proletariat as I do about chorus girls. As to Freud: He lived all his life in Vienna, a fairly compact city. Inside Vienna there was the compact Jewish community, and inside that community the compact Freud family. Freud was swaddled in triple compactness. He felt repressed, stifled, frustrated and haunted. His most natural impulses had to run a gauntlet of forebodings before they could terminate in action. On the other hand, I grew up like a stone in the field. Until 1949 there was hardly a person who knew I existed. No one watched me or expected anything from me. I was free as the wind. There were no limits and no repressions. I could as easily copulate as urinate. I could make an ass of myself or go to the dogs any time I felt like it. Yet all my life I had horrible nightmares. Was it unreasonable to assume that Freud could not possibly interpret my nightmares?

February 15, 10:00 P.M.

What will the flood of money do to the Arabs? A flood of gold hastened the decline of Spain and Portugal while the inflow of riches during the first half of the nineteenth century propelled Britain to economic and political supremacy. Money works wonders where there is an enterprising middle class continually replenished by new recruits.

60

It will be a shame if the Arabs are allowed to transmute their oil money into influence and power.

February 17, 7:30 A.M.

I was so busy yesterday that I forgot to write. I spent most of the day with the Hudson Institute people. Herman Kahn is a phenomenon. He can hold an audience for hours while speaking sotto voce. His ideas though not sensational hook into the listener's mind.

His optimism is global. Only about nine hundred million can be classified as really poor, and the reason is usually government policies. Modernization of a backward country can be financed by tourism and the money sent back by emigrant workers. The population explosion has practically stopped. Births decline automatically when a country pulls out of poverty. Inflation is on its way out. China has a healthier society than Russia. Russia's chief shortcoming, outside agriculture, is the inability to supply spare parts. The price of oil will tumble soon. There are new sources of oil everywhere. The modern world started in 1776 with America. Intellectuals have prestige in Asia but no power. A war between Russia and China is in the cards.

The connection between Islam and oil is striking people as uncanny. Herman tells the story that when Thailand started exploring for oil it was decided to begin with the Islamic district.

February 18, 6:00 A.M.

There ought to be a small book on *The Logic of Events*—its rules and regularities; and its difference from a priori logic. Here is a jumbled summary:

A priori logic assumes that poverty breeds crime, that necessity is the mother of invention, that permissive upbringing will produce self-reliant adults, that authority hampers change. The logic of events shows the opposite to be true. Rich countries have a higher crime rate than poor countries, invention is least where the pressure of necessity is greatest, permissive upbringing produces conformist adults lacking confidence, authority is crucial for the realization of drastic change.

A priori logic assumes that people will be happier when they have more. The logic of events shows that we are less dissatisfied when we lack many things than when we seem to lack but one thing. A priori logic assumes that we have less when we give part of what we have to others whereas the logic of events shows that we multiply by dividing—that we are happiest when we share our happiness with others. A priori logic says that a straight line is the shortest distance to a goal whereas in human affairs a straight line is the shortest distance to disaster.

February 19, 6:30 A.M.

Freedom from malice has been an endearing quality of American life. Is there a change taking place? Cowardice breeds malice. Do the unseemly outbursts against the entrance of Vietnamese refugees betoken a change in the national temper?

It sometimes seems that I can remember every unseemly thing I have done in my life. I do not remember the fine things.

Now and then I feel that before I am done with the world, I shall be punished for past transgressions. There is not much time left, and there is no one from whom to ask forgiveness. Yet, strangely, the more unworthy I feel, the lighter seems the burden. If I am damned already, it cannot matter much what happens to me.

February 20, 9:00 A.M.

Civilized countries fell over each other to court Hitler even as he turned Germany's Jews into pariahs. The same countries are now falling over each other to court the Arabs, who are determined to destroy Israel. The world feels no shame when it betrays Jews. It is as if fate has placed the Jews outside the comity of mankind.

The twentieth century is a Jewish century (Marx, Freud, Einstein), yet this century has seen the most fearful slaughter of Jews.

11:00 P.M.   It is an aspect of the human paradox that the attempt to transcend humanity often results in a return to animality. Post-human often means pre-human. There must be many examples of this passage from "post" to "pre." I can think of two: post-Christianity often means a return to paganism, and post-industrialism a return to pre-industrialism. There is a circularity in human affairs—if you go far enough you return to where you started. Is this because we are living on a circular planet?

February 21, 9:10 A.M.
The age of twenty-seven (give or take a year) seems to be a critical point in the lives of outstanding persons. It is the age at which they first know what they want their lifework to be. Alexis de Tocqueville felt in 1832 that his apprentice years were over and knew the great work that lay before him. It was in 1901 that Churchill decided to enter politics. Leopold von Ranke decided to switch from philology to history in 1822. In 1755 Captain James Cook refused a captaincy on a collier and entered the royal navy as an able seaman. Einstein had his first glimpse of his relativity theory in 1905. You get the approximate birthdate of these people by subtracting 27 from the dates mentioned.

To the Jews the age of 13 (the Sumerian unit of 12 plus 1) marks the threshold of adulthood. It is curious how significant multiples of 13 are in the individual's life. At 2×13 the mind catches up with the body. 3×13 marks the beginning of a change of life. At 4×13 creative people catch their second breath. 5×13 is the age of retirement, and 6×13 most often marks the end of life.

February 22, 9:30 A.M.

I have assumed that a society that cannot safeguard its young and defend its old cannot be buoyant. Yet while England was bursting with energies between 1820 and 1840 the English working people could neither protect their children nor give security to the old. The children went into mines and factories, and the old ended up in the poorhouse.

The present lethargy of the British workingman was preceded by the indolence of the British middle class at the turn of the nineteenth century. This indolence was a factor in the coming of the First World War. The hardworking Germans were getting the better of the British everywhere (January 1), and the bitter rivalry made the British receptive to the idea that Germany must be stopped.

February 23, 7:30 A.M.

The legacy of the 1960s: a revulsion from work; a horde of educated nobodies who want to be somebodies and end up being busybodies; a half-submerged counterculture of drugs and drift still able to swallow juveniles (of every age) who cannot adjust to a humdrum existence.

The sickness of the twentieth century has been cowardice—the cowardice of millions allowing themselves to be liquidated by communists and Nazis without hitting back. If every victim had done all he could to take one murderer with him, history might have been different.

Anger is the only cure for cowardice—anger strong enough to overcome fear. Right now people are afraid to get angry.

February 24, 9:15 A.M.

To learn from experience can be painful, expensive and time-consuming. The wise learn from the experience of others, and the creative know how to make a crumb of experience go a long way. The Greeks derived their theories not from experience but from looking on. The Greek *theorein* means to look on.

I have learned more from the ancient Hebrews than from the ancient Greeks. But lately I find myself preoccupied with pre-Socratic Greeks. I have the feeling that post-industrial society will have to be Greek in spirit. Industrial society with its single-minded drive and its passion to master things has its roots in the Old Testament. But a post-industrial society will not follow the injunction "Be fruitful, and multiply, and replenish the earth, and subdue it."

The Greeks had no clichés, no fictions, no vital lies. They were not afraid to face the facts of life. They had nothing to hide, nothing they wanted to escape from. Conversation was their passionate pursuit. But whereas in America the passionate pursuit of business drained energies from other departments of life, Greek conversation canalized energies into all sorts of pursuits. They were many-minded. Just as in their conversations in the agora men of every variety communed with each other, so in their minds all sorts of interests and bents intermixed. They had no specialization. The men who managed the state, fought the wars, and sailed the ships also wrote the poetry, thought the philosophy, and carved the statues.

The Greeks invented logic but were not fooled by it. They had an eye for the inner logic of events. They were close observers and based their thinking on what they observed. They had none of the clichés and platitudes mouthed by our logicians.

65

February 25, 9:45 A.M.

I was highfalutin when I said that a society needs a passion for excellence if it is to stay vigorous. Another way of putting it would be that a society stays vigorous so long as it can educe dedication and craftsmanship from the people it pays well to do the world's work.

In human affairs a device or a policy is most successful when rendered invisible. Changes are most successful when they are scarcely perceived. A successful manager makes management invisible, and authority is most potent when hidden in hearts and minds.

Different ways of saying the same thing:

TOLSTOI: "Every man can be seen as a fraction whose numerator is his actual qualities and its denominator his opinion of himself."

BISMARCK: "Every man is the sum of his qualities minus his vanity."

My own (in *Reflections on the Human Condition*): "A man's worth is what he is divided by what he thinks he is."

Poets are held in high repute in Russia and often feared by government not because of the power of poetry to move and shape souls but because, in Russia, only great poets dare speak the truth.

February 26, 6:30 A.M.

The societies of ants and bees are made possible by the total instinctuality of every ant and bee. On the other hand, human society is made possible by the fact that the young of the human species hardly possess any instincts, and have to be taught everything. It is this teaching that develops the emotional reactions which lie at the base of social life.

Both the ancient Greeks and Chinese had an exaggerated idea of the power of music. Pythagoras used music as a medicine to purge souls. To Plato, a change in music was a prelude to social change. Do we know anything about Greek music?

According to Confucius: "The spirit of a community is formed by the music it hears. Hence a government must encourage one kind of music and forbid another." When one of his disciples became the governor of a city, he instructed the people in music as a first principle of government.

Singing together reinforces social cohesion. For some reason the Russians, the Germans and the Welsh are good at mass singing.

February 27, 9:00 A.M.
   Last night I dreamed about God—a gray-haired old man with bloodshot eyes surrounded by commissars. Something had been completed, and he came down to inspect. He looked tired. The commissars kept repeating: "They ought to love us."

No one has said worse things about the Russians than the Russians themselves. Russia's chronic despotism has its roots in the boundless contempt for the Russian people which possessed anyone who had power over them. A recurrent epithet in the expressions of contempt is "deceitful savages." Dostoevski believed that Russians are most easily won over "by an open advocacy of a right to be dishonorable."

The East's influence on the West (December 27): It was in the eighteenth century that the Eastern tea-drinking habit spread to the English-speaking peoples and eventually was a factor in the outbreak of the American Revolution. It was also in the eighteenth century that fine Indian cottons became so fashionable that they threatened domestic manufacturing of woolens and silks.

To Eisenhower, an intellectual is "a man who takes more words than are necessary to tell more than he knows." As President, Eisenhower mastered the art of saying nothing at great length—he used more words than were necessary to say less than he knew.

February 28, 2:10 P.M.
Right now in every country not under communist rule a high percentage of the intellectuals are contemptuous of capitalism. The fact that in capitalist countries most intellectuals are fairly well off—that they often combine anti-capitalist opinions with capitalist bank accounts—only serves to fan their hostility. Their influence has been increasing since Sputnik. They are brainwashing politicians, civil servants, judges, editors, publishers, journalists, teachers, students, broadcasters and even "concerned" businessmen. It is obvious that a capitalist society must know how to deal effectively with its would-be destroyers if it is to survive. But it is difficult to see how a society can fight its educated classes.

To Max Beloff, a sagacious, fair-minded scholar (Oxford), the Bolshevik Revolution remains the major catastrophe of the twentieth century. It is "the breach in the walls of civilization through which so many hordes of barbarians have poured and are pouring." He feels that "the world has been a poorer, bleaker, and more dangerous place because Lenin lived."

March 1, 8:00 A.M.
It will need a new type of businessman to cope with the writers, artists, scholars and so on who are increasingly shaping our attitude toward business. I have suggested (February 11) that potential poets and philosophers originally gave American business its Promethean sweep and drive, and it may take culture-bearing businessmen—as much at home in

literary and artistic circles as in board rooms—to guide business at present.

Up to the First World War neither Britain nor America underestimated its strength. In France there was overestimation. The democracies lost their nerve after the war, and it was the underestimation of their strength that made possible the rise of Hitler and the coming of the Second World War.

During the Second World War Britain and America courted Stalin, who needed them more than they needed him. Even after America's superb performance in the Pacific, Roosevelt did not believe we could defeat Japan without Russian help.

Right now Israel is the only democracy that does not underestimate its strength, and it is being warned by the Western democracies that overconfidence may endanger its survival.

Logicians are baffled by the logic of events (February 18), which upsets their predictions. They tend to see it as a mysterious, even spiteful, power. Hegel spoke of "the cunning of history." René Grousset saw a mocking demiurge playing tricks behind the scenes and delighting in drawing from men's actions consequences least foreseen.

Henry George remarked on the fact that the excellent mind that conceived and built the Brooklyn Bridge could not prevent a lot of condemned wire from getting into the bridge. As I said before, the human mind is at its best mastering things but seems awkward when coping with men.

March 2, 6:50 A.M.

It was a symptom of the Occident's failure of nerve that hardly anyone foresaw Europe's rapid recovery after the Second World War. No one believed that Germany would rise from the rubble in less than fifty years. We so underestimate ourselves that we do not use our strength even when it is a question of survival, as in the energy crisis. It is an ugly spectacle to see the Western democracies fall over each other to sell their souls for a barrel of oil. The radical-chic loudmouths are blubbing about the "disutility of force." They say that when a democracy flexes its muscles it acts against the Zeitgeist. The same people see violence by criminals as revolutionary, and a vigorous reaction against crime as vigilantism.

It would be safer for the Occident to be reckless and make mistakes than to be fearful and sink into inaction.

The educated classes: On the one hand a large number of educated people who want to live important lives. They cannot find fulfillment in making a good living by doing their share of the world's work. And they lack the humility and patience which might enable them to achieve distinction by realizing their capacities and talents.

On the other hand, there are a number of creative, prestigious individuals—scholars, writers, artists, scientists—who are adverse to the practical, materialist temper of capitalist society. They are contemptuous of the triviality and banality of the marketplace. They want a society in which souls are stretched by grandiose tasks and noble challenges.

How is capitalist society to deal with them? I am playing with an idea that is perhaps impractical but which I find attractive: to find grandiose tasks for the educated by having them do the things capitalist society cannot do.

I have to chew on this some more.

March 3, 9:00 A.M.

The elegant way to solve problems is to put one problem to solve another. You solve the problem of adversary educated classes by giving the educated a chance to solve some of the problems capitalism cannot solve.

Capitalism is ideal for people who can take care of themselves but it cannot do much for the helpless. Capitalism cannot cure chronic poverty, cannot do much for the old, and cannot ease the passage of adolescents to adulthood. My suggestion is that the educated classes should be given a free hand and the required means to deal with the helpless, and in the process find the high drama and grandiose challenges that would quicken their spirits.

There should be an enclave wholly in the keeping of the intelligentsia—perhaps a whole state run by professors, students, writers, artists. They will probably fashion a communal society. The chronically poor will be settled in cooperative hamlets, where they will be taught to produce vegetables, fruit, eggs and milk. Juveniles will become members of large kibbutzim engaged in both agriculture and industry. The old too will live in a communal milieu, where they will find a sense of usefulness and opportunities to learn and grow. Finally, the temporarily unemployed will be given plots of ground on which to grow vegetables, and be encouraged to hunt and fish.

The communal state will not be cut off from the rest of the country. Those who weary of the rat race will be free to transfer to the new state. It is also possible that once the chronically poor become self-reliant they may choose to return to the free-swinging capitalist society. The same might be true of the adolescents who attain manhood, and of the unemployed who are offered jobs.

4:00 P.M.   Bought a shirt, cigars, and tobacco. Spent a fortune and feeling fine. Can't tell why.

10:15 P.M.   The shirt is shoddy. The buttonholes are frayed and there are loose folds of cloth inside. I shall drop the thing in hot water and hope it dissolves.

March 4, 6:00 A.M.
At the Congress of Vienna, Prussia was considered more Slavic than German. (The names Prussia, Pomerania, Silesia and even Berlin are Slavic.) Yet it was this partly non-German state that unified Germany.

71

All through history, outsiders played crucial roles. Moses, Disraeli, Napoleon, Hitler and Stalin were outsiders. The glory of Athens at its height was due as much to the achievements of outsiders as to those of native Athenians. The Arab renaissance was largely the work of outsiders—Persians, Greeks, Turks, Jews, and Spaniards. Al Kindi was the only purely Arab philosopher.

The eighteenth century was the golden age of the intellectuals. They were feared and courted by the mighty. Frederick the Great courted Voltaire, and Catherine the Great went to great lengths to woo Diderot. Frederick and Catherine feared Voltaire's and Diderot's power to shape European opinion. One wonders whether the heads of large business corporations would take the trouble and be as skillful wooing the intellectuals who are shaping America's attitude toward business.

March 5, 8:45 A.M.
On the threshold of the twentieth century, two Jews—Theodor Herzl and the English Rabbi Moses Gaster—foresaw the coming of a dark age.

Herzl in an address to Lord Rothschild in 1897: "It is impossible to hope that the Jewish position will improve. If I am asked how I know it, I should say that I can tell you where a stone rolling down an inclined plane will go—right to the bottom. . . . I cannot foretell the forms it will take. Will it be expropriation through revolution from below or confiscation by reactionary forces from above? In some countries they will drive us out, while in others they will slay us. Is there no way out?"

Rabbi Gaster (in a symposium, *The Great Religions of the World*, Harper, 1901): "A mighty wind of reaction is blowing over all Europe. We are moving on a downward plane leading from equality, fraternity, freedom and right to racial hatred, national exclusiveness, military brutalization . . . from the free and serene atmosphere of human faith to the swamps of mysticism, occultism; to the inquisition and the stake."

About the same time, the Zionist leader Max Nordau predicted that beautiful socialism would end in anti-Semitism: "If we should live to see theory become practice you'll be surprised to meet again in the new order that old acquaintance anti-Semitism, and it won't help at all that Marx and Lassalle were Jews."

March 6, 7:00 A.M.

In preceding entries I pointed out the almost total un-awareness of impending catastrophe in the decades before the First World War. I quoted among others the German Jewish writer Stefan Zweig (January 18), who said that he had never had more faith in the future than in the years before the war. Herzl, Rabbi Gaster and Nordau were poignantly Jewish, and never recovered from the shock of the Dreyfus affair. Zweig, on the other hand, saw himself as an outstanding German writer and a European. His suicide in 1942 suggests an inability to draw strength from an identification with the Jewish people.

What I cannot understand is the blindness of the German Jews during the 1920s and the early 1930s. There was the widespread delusion that the Russian Revolution and Weimar Germany had created a new climate of enlightenment. The German Jews refused to take Hitler seriously until it was too late. They had not an inkling of what the average German felt and thought. They could not see, as Jung did, that Hitler "magnified the inaudible whispers of the German soul"; that he was articulating what Germans had been thinking since the defeat of the First World War.

The blindness of the German Jews strikes me as a mark of decadence. It will fare ill with Jews everywhere if they allow the memory of Hitler's holocaust to be blurred during the remainder of this terrible century.

March 7, 8:15 A.M.

The situation in Britain: Has there ever been such a striking example of the evanescence of greatness? It seems unacceptable that in less than a lifetime Great Britain should become a fairly contented small country. The causes of Britain's economic and political decline are present in all advanced countries, and though they need not inevitably lead to a loss of greatness they are likely to result in a new style of life.

A Britain that chooses leisure and a rich cultural life over goods might serve as a model for advanced countries that have entered the post-industrial age without clear ideas about the new possibilities and goals. The pity of it is that, at present, Britain lacks the economic base to support the good life. The poor performance of labor and management makes British exports non-competitive. Might it be possible for British excellence in science, art, literature and technical invention to create a market for cultural exports?

March 8, 7:50 A.M.

France will never recover from her experience during the German occupation. It was not so much a defeat as a lancing of a spiritual boil. The air was poisoned by the stench of a putrefying vainglorious culture. Robert Brasillach, a shining light of French culture, said in 1942 in connection with the rounding up of Jewish children: "We have got to get rid of the Jews as a whole and not keep the children."

France will remain hostile toward any manifestation of courage in the free world. She will go on courting enemies and scorning friends. She will welcome abuse of the Occident from any quarter and celebrate the retreat of Western civilization in the backward world.

March 9, 6:00 A.M.

Greek individual freedom was not a by-product of a stalemate between two coercive powers (Church and State), as it was in the West, but the result of a fortuitous break with coercive patterns of the past. The Dorian invasion, early in the first millennium B.C., washed remnants of shattered communities and tribes onto the shores of Ionia. This mixed multitude was almost without a memory of the past.

What was it that generated in the Greeks a creative tension? They were the first free men immersed in a sea of barbarism. Without the binding power of dogmatic religion and traditional patriotism, their society hovered on the brink of anarchy. They had to search for the foundations of the beliefs, customs and attitudes indispensable for a stable social existence. Everything had to be discussed and analyzed. There were few things they could take for granted.

March 10, 7:15 A.M.

Those who rate heredity higher than environment in the shaping of a society have a lot of explaining to do. They have to account for the long periods of stagnation and the usually brief outbursts of creativity. You cannot attribute the petering out of Periclean Athens or of the fabulous era of Dutch painting to a loss of genes. Someone said that heredity proposes and environment disposes, which is a way of saying that environment is decisive.

It seems that societies immersed in action are not likely to produce great writers, painters, composers or even great scientists. America after the Civil War was seething with energies yet its literature, art and science were anemic. So too the rapid industrialization of Imperial Germany after 1870 went hand in hand with a cultural decline. Germany's greatest literary age, 1760–1830, was an age of economic and political stagnation. The greatest Russian writers, composers and scientists made their appearance in stagnant Czarist Russia just as the phenomenal intellectual and artistic vitality of Vienna at the turn of the century was the product of a stagnant Hapsburg empire. The most striking association between creative vigor and social stagnation is of course the flowering of Classical Greece at a time when Athens was in economic and political decline. We also know (December 27) that at the height of the Renaissance Italian banking and trade were losing their paramount position in Europe and the Mediterranean countries.

Still, the relation between action and creativeness may not be as automatic as I have made it out to be. Through most of history, general stagnation was the rule—absence of action was concurrent with an absence of cultural activity. It is also conceivable that in a society bursting with energies action and creativeness may, under certain conditions, go hand in hand.

March 11, 10:00 A.M.

1550 to 1650 was a century of great literature in both Spain and England although economically and politically England was on the rise and Spain in accelerated decline. Could there be perhaps a difference between insular and continental patterns of energy? In Elizabethan England the rule did not hold that opportunities for impressive action draw energies away from cultural pursuits. So too in the first half of the nineteenth century the unprecedented opportunities for action opened by the industrial revolution did not leave English literature anemic. On the contrary, this age of economic and political expansion became one of the greatest poetical epochs in England's history. It was the age of Wordsworth, Byron, Shelley, Keats, Coleridge, Browning, Tennyson and others. The literary output outweighed in volume and value that of any other period.

It is of interest that England's insular pattern seems to have been carried over to New England, and persisted there until the middle of the nineteenth century. With the opening of the West in the 1850s the familiar continental pattern made its appearance. The cultural flowering of New England came to an abrupt end when potential writers, artists, scholars and philosophers went off to seek their fortunes in mining, railroading, manufacturing and the like.

Finally, it seems that Britain's decline signals the loss of its insular uniqueness. The present economic and political crisis is due partly to the fact that Britain's finest brains and energies are going into universities and cultural pursuits. We are seeing the association of economic and political stagnation with undiminished creativeness in literature, music and science.

March 12, 7:15 A.M.

Yesterday I received an invitation from Herman Kahn to attend a seminar on the prospects of mankind to be held at Rockefeller University in New York. The truth is that I am not interested in the prospects of mankind but in the prospects of families—few of them without tragedies.

1:30 P.M.   The idea of insular and continental patterns of energy does not stand up. France, a continental country, offers the example of an even creative flow unaffected by the oscillations of the economic or political pendulum. The reason is probably that in no other country are writers and artists so admired and honored. There is the story about Clemenceau breaking up a cabinet meeting when told that Monet had become dejected and stopped painting the water lilies in the Louvre. Clemenceau rushed to cheer him up and get him painting again. One cannot see a President of the United States interrupting a Cabinet meeting to call up a despairing Hemingway and perhaps save him from suicide.

Ortega y Gasset when exiled from Spain wandered alone through the streets of Paris, where he knew not a soul, only to discover that he was surrounded by old friends, the statues of writers and thinkers he had known all his life, and he could now discuss with them, face to face, the great problems of mankind. An American writer who lived in Paris tells how the neighborhood grocer and baker who knew he was writing a book treated him as they would a woman big with child.

March 13, 7:20 A.M.

Last night I spoke to an audience of common people, half of them black. I told them, among other things, that if they believed in God they must know that he loved them since he made so many of them. He is also a just God. Hence it would be blasphemous to assume that a loving, just God showered all His gifts on a chosen few and left our minds and hearts empty and shrunken. We are actually richer than we think. God has implanted in us the seed of all greatness and it is up to us to see that the seed germinates and grows. Learning and growing should be a kind of worship. For God has given us capacities and talents and it is our sacred duty to finish God's work.

Many have remarked on the capacity of popular opinion to foretell events. The unlearned apply what they see around them to the affairs of the great world. I heard an illiterate longshoreman predict on V-J Day that America would soon be quarreling with Russia, citing the behavior of boys playing on a sandlot. It has been my impression that the unlearned can read the book of the world better than the learned.

March 14, 6:45 A.M.

Khrushchev spoke of Russia's agricultural and industrial output as "the battering ram with which to stave in capitalist society." Right now American farmers and industrialists are using America's agricultural and industrial output to prop up the Soviet system. It is preposterous that we should have to defend capitalist society against capitalist schoolboys (December 23) collaborating with bloody-minded communist schoolmasters.

According to Bergson "the intellect is characterized by an inability to comprehend life." Kant was certain that "the origin of the cosmos will be explained sooner than the mechanism of a plant or a caterpillar." How outlandish is then the belief that the intellect can fathom man's soul.

How can science unravel the chemistry of the soul when what we have here is actually an alchemy? Good and evil, beauty and ugliness, truth and error, love and hatred, the sublime and the ridiculous continually pass into each other. And alchemy is ruled not by the intellect but by magic.

March 15, 6:20 A.M.

Last night we had dinner at Tommy's Joynt and saw *Stavisky*. The French do not produce unalloyed villains. In this they resemble the Old Testament. Stavisky, played by Belmondo, comes through as a vigorous human being who dominates without coercion. His vigorous appetites, like exceptional talents, gave him the belief that the world was his oyster. The film is about social corruption and decadence, yet it has not a single loathsome or obscene episode.

We need a sense of grandeur. Were I an architect I would give every public building, even a post office, a lofty ceiling, soaring columns, marble floors—and tack utility onto the grandeur. We need the frequent enactment of grandiose public ceremonies. My feeling is that it is vital for democratic societies at present to cultivate the grandiose the way churches and monarchies did in the past.

I find it comforting that Lenin, Stalin and Hitler were not memorable in what they said—that they were not "wise."

It has always amazed me that men of action should be more quotable than thinkers and writers. I am thinking of Frederick the Great, Napoleon, Wellington, Disraeli, Bismarck, Churchill, de Gaulle, Adenauer. Henry Ford is the only quotable businessman I can think of. And what of FDR? He never said anything worth remembering. Could it be that he had not heard clever conversation in his youth—not even the pithy remarks of common people?

March 16, 7:40 A.M.

Cleansing souls is risky. Bizet declared that "if you suppress adultery, fanaticism, crime, fallacy, the supernatural, there is no more means of writing a note." Montaigne saw our being so cemented by sickly qualities that "whoever should divest men of them would destroy the fundamental conditions of human life." Sir Francis Bacon had no doubt that "if there were taken out of men's minds vain opinions, flattering hopes, false valuations and the like, it would leave the minds of men poor, shrunken things." Renan feared that we can get rid of the bad only at the sacrifice of what is excellent, remarkable and extraordinary.

The proponents of reason who set their hearts on cleansing souls of the irrational released demonic forces beyond control of reason.

Capitalism is in trouble because of its belief that everyone can take care of himself. It does not know how to help those who cannot help themselves. On the other hand, socialism is in trouble because it believes that no one can take care of himself.

Except the love for a child, all love is flawed. All that one can say of love is that it enables us to put up wholeheartedly with imperfections. This is true also of self-love.

March 17, 8:45 A.M.
        It seems to be true that all great events come unheralded. I cannot think of a war or a revolution that did not come as a surprise. The fact that the Second World War was expected marks it as a continuation of the First World War. It seems incredible that the industrial revolution, one of the greatest events in history, was not foreseen by anyone. No one forecast the development of a machine industry.

It was not long ago that national greatness seemed a legitimate goal for almost any country. At present, a deliberate reaching out for national greatness is not found outside Russia and China. It is curious that at a time when every two-bit intellectual in a democratic country wants to make history, the free world has become skeptical of great feelings and sacrifices. The democracies aspire not to historical greatness but to the attainment of a modicum of material prosperity. Will this retreat of the free world from greatness make the world ripe for universal Russian dominion?

March 18, 6:40 A.M.

I cannot think of anything more un-Oriental than the first chapters of Genesis. The theorizing is in the grand scientific style even though the theories are based on fictions rather than facts.

A case can be made out that the ancient Hebrews were the first Occidentals. In the Orient power has always been absolute, as implacable as a force of nature. The Hebrews invented the division of power—between kings and prophets and later between Pharisees and the secular power. Finally, it was the Hebrew influence that created the tension that stretched Occidental souls, and generated the Occident's unique dynamism. Greek-dominated Byzantium knew no separation between Church and State, and became an Oriental despotism. I remember reading somewhere that in both Byzantium and Russia the Old Testament did not enter the lives of the pious as it did in the West.

One hears a lot about the primacy of Greek influence in the shaping of the Occident. But Greek influence flowed eastward, to Antioch, Alexandria, Persia and all the way to the borders of India. Until the fall of Constantinople Greek influence reached Europe through Arab channels. On the other hand, Hebrew influence penetrated Europe directly after the birth of Christianity and the destruction of the Second Temple. The Hebrews turned their backs on the Orient.

However vital the Greek heritage has been for the Occident's science, art and literature, it did not enter the lives of the people. The Occident's temper has been not Greek but Hebrew, and much of what is good and bad in us has Hebraic

81

roots. And when Europeans crossed the Atlantic to possess the new world they carried not the Greek but the Hebrew heritage with them. It was Jehovah's injunction to subdue the earth that sustained the pioneers in their attempt to tame a savage continent in an incredibly short time. Greek learning came later. It was brought over by scholars and remained confined to houses of learning.

Still, as I have suggested (February 24), it could well be that if the post-industrial era evolves a new style of life it may follow the Greek model.

March 19, 8:30 A.M.

Even when I force myself to appreciate what is good in communist Russia—the spread of education and the modernization of the Central Asian states and of Siberia—I keep remembering de Custine's belief that providence created Russia not to diminish the barbarism of Asia but to chastise Europe. I cannot help feeling that Russia is destined to destroy Western civilization.

Stalin suspected his closest comrades but trusted Hitler. I wonder whether this is partly explained by the fact that in Eastern Europe no one trusts a Russian, but Germans, even when disliked, are held in high repute for their probity, cleanliness, efficiency and learning.

No similarity is so genuinely similar as a difference is different. Most of the time an insistence on similarities is an attempt to evade thinking, whereas a probing of differences is almost always seminal. Our understanding of Russia is not furthered by the assumption that Russians are like everybody else. It might be intellectually more profitable to go to the other extreme and assume that the Russians are a species apart. The acceptance of fundamental differences would not only make us better observers of Russian behavior but might make our dealings with the Russians less frustrating by moderating our expectations.

March 20, 7:15 A.M.

In Soviet Russia scientists, ballet dancers, musical virtuosi and chess players often achieve excellence while writers and artists remain on the whole mediocre. The reason is not mainly that writers and artists are more under the thumb of the censor. Even without censorship literature and art will not thrive where there are no friendship, no free conversation, no shame and no extravagant dreams. Moreover, science, ballet and so on live each in its own world while literature and art derive their nourishment from the social milieu.

The middle class is the only revolutionary class in history—the only class that accepts and promotes ceaseless change. The middle-class revolution changes not only a country's technology but its physical appearance and its way of life. Revolutions by other classes—by aristocrats, intellectuals, soldiers—change fundamentally little and terminate in stagnation. When, as in Britain at the turn of the century, the middle class embraces aristocratic values, it loses its revolutionary ferment and tends toward stagnation.

How has middle-class domination affected the human spirit? It has brought unrest, frustration, tension, insecurity, triviality and insatiable desire. It has also brought unimagined affluence and given rise to great literature, art and science. Middle-class domination stretched but did not cripple the human spirit.

March 21, 10:00 A.M.

I have set out a dish of bird seed and a basin of water on the balcony. I no longer have any illusion about birdlike innocence. One bully gets into the dish and drives off all other birds. The bullies seem demented and malicious. They skip about pecking at other birds rather than eat the seed. Why don't the birds gang up on the bully? Is it because of a lack of language? Birds are capable of united action: they flock together and organize themselves into flights to the ends of the earth.

It wearies me to think that the senseless pecking is part of the energy that fueled the ascent of life—the manifestation of a tireless, blind drive that will go on forever.

It occurs to me that only birds, two-legged creatures, can simulate human speech. Nothing that crawls or walks on four legs can utter words. The snake who spoke to Adam and Eve walked erect. He became mute when made to crawl. "Upon thy belly shalt thou go."

How did the snake manage to walk erect? Probably with the aid of hummingbird wings. He must have been a proud sight. To me, the story of the fall is above all the story of the fall of the snake.

March 22, 6:25 A.M.

It is doubtful whether writers and artists will ever be worshiped as they were during the Renaissance and the 1700s. One cannot see present-day presidents, prime ministers or bankers vie for the favor of Leonardo, Raphael, Michelangelo, Erasmus, Voltaire and Diderot. The worship had a religious quality. Both the Renaissance and the eighteenth century were preceded by periods of intense religious devotion. The habit of adoration lingered on but was transferred to non-religious objects. When religious intensity returned with the Reformation and Counter-Reformation the adoration of writers and artists subsided. It reappeared when religiosity was discredited by the excesses of the Thirty Years' War.

Thucydides quotes Cleon that "Ordinary men usually arrange public affairs better than their more gifted fellows." It is something I have known all along (December 23).

Why should ordinary people be better organizers than people who feel themselves above the average? Ordinary people have more trust in their fellow men, and trust is a precondition for effective organizing. It is also true that ordinary people are never certain that they know best, hence their willingness to listen and compromise. Finally, ordinary people are not likely to demand perfection and will settle for the possible.

March 23, 7:45 A.M.

The Jewish refugees from Russia are on the whole unenterprising and seem unfit for a free society. The contrast with the Jewish refugees from Hitler's Germany is striking. The German Jews brought with them wherever they went a creative ferment. They contributed to economic and cultural growth in Israel, Britain and the Americas. They did not expect special treatment. The Russian refugees are confused and lost in a free environment.

The difference between the aftermaths of the First and the Second World War may be explained by the fact that the First World War was not over until the end of the Second. It was only then that European nationalism lost its virulence and enemies became friends. Still, one wonders whether with a strong France at the end of the Second World War and in the absence of a Russian threat the aftermath would have been what it was.

March 24, 8:30 A.M.

According to Paul Valéry, no great power in modern times has been able to hold on to its conquests for more than fifty years. Should this be true, Russia's day of judgment will come in the 1990s. Yet the staying power of the colossus seems awesome. Russia seems large and rich enough to weather any crisis. It may well continue more or less unchanged despite the chronic inefficiency of its economy and the anti-human absurdities of its system. However, if Russia's day does come, everyone will wonder that few people foresaw the inevitable end. The final breakup of a clumsy conglomerate of a hundred nationalities situated between nine hundred million irreconcilable Chinese and millions of resentful colonial subjects in Eastern Europe will seem to have been foreordained.

It is generally agreed that, at present, countries are more threatened by enemies within than without. Yet there are no accepted methods for coping with internal enemies. When an external enemy breaks the peace there is a state of war and an automatic mobilization of armed forces. But when internal enemies disrupt a country's life by bombing and killing there is no state of emergency. The courts go on grinding out decisions, the police stick to their routine, and the majority remains silent. Only in some Latin American countries have internal disorders led to a state of war between the armed forces and the violent minorities. We see such a response as anomalous and tend to label organized defense against internal enemies as oppression. Nevertheless, we may eventually follow the Latin American example. The world is increasingly being Latin Americanized.

March 25, 6:00 A.M.
    The fundamental difference between the thinker and the artist is that the thinker looks for a universal truth that will help explain unique events while the artist endows the unique with an intimation of the universal. What they have in common is that to both the visible is mysterious.

Things I cannot understand: the passion for immortality; the delusion that there is a cure for all the world's ills; Hitler's rise to power; the morbid hatred of some intellectuals for America; the belief of many people that good things will come to pass without effort; that so many well-educated people consider Lenin a great man.

86

They have been doing it all the time: they raze Bastilles and raise Kremlins.

The early settlers must have often felt that this savage continent was ruled by alien, hostile Gods who lashed out at mankind with snowstorms, sandstorms, tornadoes and floods. They needed a Jehovah who had created man and appointed him His viceroy on earth to sustain them. Even now in the Middle West when nature vents its fury in awe-inspiring electric storms, there must be a vague fear of hostile powers in the upper regions communing with each other and plotting against man.

Only a society that knows how to socialize juveniles may spoil children with impunity. Where a society lacks the confidence and the will to fashion adolescents in its image, permissive child rearing may have catastrophic consequences. The Japanese, who know how to force adolescents into a strait jacket of prescribed behavior, can afford to indulge and spoil children up to the age of eight or nine.

Spiritual stagnation ensues either when man's environment becomes unpredictable or when his inner life is made wholly predictable. In Stalin's Russia the social environment was unpredictable: one never knew what might happen between going to bed and getting up. At the same time, terror and indoctrination made Russians as predictable as minerals.

March 26, 9:15 A.M.

It would be an understatement to say that the world has treated me better than I deserve. I have been favored by chance and treated royally by circumstances. Moreover, I have been spared both envy and greed.

It never bothered me that there are people who live in fabulous opulence. And I never assumed that to be rich is to be happy. However, the present galloping inflation is darkening my view of the rich. They are getting richer while the value of the few dollars I have saved is melting away. Should I live a few more years, I may have to pinch pennies in my last days. The rich raise prices in order to maintain a steady increase of profits. The rich are not paying taxes. There is not a law the rich and their shyster lawyers cannot get around. On Friday, April 4, I have to speak to a group of lawyers. I shall speak of the sins of the rich.

I am reading Nietzsche's letters. I used to be scornful of his pathological vanity—he actually expected an earthquake every time he had a new idea. But now I am overcome with compassion. The man was losing his mind. Reading about his breakdown in Turin in 1889, I suddenly saw the soul-wrenching predicament of a great spirit who needs a state of exaltation to do his best. An addiction to ecstasy may lead to madness and self-destruction.

I have always equated individual as well as social health with the ability to perform well at room temperature.

Yesterday I was accosted by a young fellow who wanted to talk about crime. He was full of clichés but quite intelligent. I happened to mention that during the Great Depression most of us were poor yet the crime rate was low. He reacted quickly: It was precisely because most people were poor that there was no increase in crime. When someone is poor today, he feels poor in a rich society. I tried to show him that the assumption that poverty is the cause of crime, like the assumption that necessity is the mother of invention, is a cliché not based on fact. In both crime and invention there are elements of sport and play.

6:00 P.M.   A rare electric storm. Thunder, lightning and an angry north wind whipping the rain across the balcony almost to the glass wall. The barely visible docks below remind me of ceaseless toil, short lives and brooding eternity.

March 27, 8:30 A.M.

I am rereading Whitehead's conversations with Lucien Price. I first read the *Dialogues* about twenty years ago. They impress me less now, but they read easily. Whitehead dwells on the break at the turn of the century. When he came to Cambridge in the 1880s nearly everything was supposed to be known about physics that could be known. By the middle of the 1890s there were a few tremors but no one sensed what was coming. By 1900 Newtonian physics was demolished. Still, it is clear that the upheaval in science had no immediate effect on the Occident's intellectual and social climate.

His unqualified reverence for Plato makes me uneasy. In all my years I have not been able to make myself read Plato and learn from him directly. I started many times but never finished any of his books.

Whitehead also had not an inkling of what Russia was like. It is amazing how much more clearsighted the unlearned have been on this subject.

In the city of Antwerp in 1560 there were three times as many working artists as there were butchers. The butchers had an exclusive union and a strict pattern of apprenticeship. Only the few could become butchers but every mother's son could become a painter.

Sixteenth-century Antwerp was a compact neighborhood, where children could watch artists at work. Tales about the fame and fortune of great painters were known to all. Becoming a painter was no more beyond reach than becoming a baseball player is today. Appreciation of art in sixteenth-century Antwerp was probably as diffused as the appreciation of baseball is in an American city.

Aristotle Onassis died recently of pneumonia contracted in the hospital after a bladder operation. Hospitals are becoming dangerous places. Negligence is a malady of our time and it seems as prevalent in hospitals as in factories.

March 28, 11:00 A.M.

Was Christianity a factor in the release of Jewish energies? In the non-Christian world the Jews sank to the level of the natives, both intellectually and economically. It is true that during the Moslem renaissance the Jews were in the van, but they declined with the Moslems after A.D. 1200. On the other hand, the Jews preserved their intellectual prowess in the inert Christian world of the Middle Ages, and later in the stagnant atmosphere of Eastern Europe. In the eighteenth century, in dark, illiterate Lithuania, the Jews produced the great Rabbi Elijah Ben Solomon, the "Gaon" of Vilna.

With emancipation at the turn of the eighteenth century, the pent-up Jewish energies burst over central and western Europe and contributed, disproportionately, to the fabulous economic and scientific expansion initiated by the industrial revolution. This was particularly true in Germany. One wonders what would have happened had the Jewish energies been canalized eastward and given free play in the vast expanse of Russia. The question is whether the Jews could have performed in Russia as they did in Germany.

March 29, 6:00 A.M.

When I read what Paul Valéry wrote about the Occident after the First World War I am surprised by its contemporaneity. It is as if he were writing about the 1970s. This reminds me of de Custine's description of Russia in the 1840s, which strikes me as a description of the Stalin era. It is as if we predict the future when we exaggerate the defects of the present.

Had Britain kept out of the First World War there would have been no Hitler, no Second World War and no Russians on the Elbe. The decline of the West would have been delayed for at least a century. There are those who say that Britain would have lost its soul had it not entered the war. But what we have now after two ruinously victorious World Wars is a Britain with not too much soul and without balls.

Senility consists partly in not being able to take things for granted. The old are not sure that their legs will carry them, their arms will lift, their eyes will see, their stomach will digest. Would this be true also of a society? Does a society become senile when it no longer can take familiar practices and attitudes for granted?

March 30, 7:15 A.M.
How do things look to the men in the Kremlin? Communism is spreading like leprosy. It has just now spread to Portugal and the Portuguese colonies. The Occident is in disarray, starved for energy and raw materials, and with unruly populations unwilling to work. All the men in the Kremlin have to do is sit tight. China is not an immediate threat.

Is there anyone crazy enough to believe that the West will attack Russia? Still, it is true that a prosperous Occident must trouble Russia and keep her off balance. The Occident constitutes a non-military threat against which there is no defense. Russia has not diminished its garrison in Europe by one man despite the fact that it keeps a million men on the frontier of China. The military posture in Europe has little to do with a possible threat from the West. It stems rather from Russia's vital need to look overwhelmingly strong wherever it faces the Occident—not to intimidate the Occident but to reassure Russia.

Modern manufacturers invent a product and then find a use for it. Psychoanalysis tries to induce the disease for which it offers itself as a cure. The revolutionary strives to produce the evils he denounces in order to apply the cure he prescribes. We have here three different human types resorting to a similar strategy. Do they perhaps respond to a similar need—the need for a sense of usefulness? No one in modern times can savor usefulness the way people did when going to bed on a full stomach was a triumph. We have now to invent uses in order to feel useful.

March 31, 9:40 A.M.

It seems to me that deeds do not bite deeply into the mind. I doubt whether people can become incurably damaged by what they do. I believe it is possible to do the terrible things many Germans did in Hitler's time and still lead a decent life afterward. It is possible to blur or completely wipe out the memory of evil deeds. Remorse is not what moralist logicians make it out to be.

Actually, it is the things we have missed doing that are likely to fester in the mind.

Yesterday we had several members of the New York City Ballet for breakfast at Lili's house. Jacques d'Amboise, the leader, is intelligent, alert and articulate. He is past forty and his dancing days are numbered. He will make an excellent teacher. He attributes the dedication and excellence of the ballet in Russia to the inhumanity and misery of the Russian world at large. It is only within the enclave of the ballet that life becomes wholesome again, free of suspicion, malice and cowardice.

April 1, 7:45 A.M.

I am dipping into David's Caute's *Fellow Travellers.* It is difficult to avoid feeling contempt for the intellectual establishment when one reads what outstanding writers and thinkers said and wrote about Stalin and the purge trials. I was in my thirties at the time, an uninformed migratory worker. Nevertheless, I knew what was going on in Russia. The same was true of most of my fellow migratory workers. Robert Conquest sees it as the misfortune of the intelligentsia that its most vocal and wrong-headed section has been taken as its representative and plenipotentiary. Actually, intellectuals of every grade of excellence were following the line laid down by the loud-mouths, afraid to dissent lest they be labeled as reactionary and fascist. And they are still doing it now on the questions of race, the events in Chile and the like.

David Caute is a master entertainer. In all the sprawling book there is not a page that drags. Of course, the material is full of interest. He gives thumbnail biographies of many people I have heard about much of my life. I would like to read essays by Caute on Plato and Hegel.

April 2, 9:15 A.M.

Democracies are naked. Anyone can see their weaknesses and shortcomings, whereas their hidden strengths can only be guessed at. The Japanese had every right to believe that hedonistic, undisciplined Americans would be no match for the fanatically dedicated Japanese warriors. Many knowledgeable Americans thought so too. It is quite natural to underestimate democracies, and it is not a mark of decadence when a democracy underestimates its own strength.

Of the outstanding achievements of German culture during its greatest flowering (1760–1830), music and philosophy had a universal appeal whereas literature, despite the monumental works of Goethe, Schiller, Lessing and others, did not reach a world audience. German music and philosophy are still potent today.

What are the universal elements in other cultures? Art, cuisine and women's fashions in France; literature and parliamentary government in Britain; business, the democratic way of life, jazz and juvenile culture in America; literature and ideology in Russia. Jewish influence is universal in commerce, science and, with the emergence of Israel, in the art of survival.

It is remarkable that, unlike in the past, small countries do not produce universal models in either the spiritual or the practical sphere (December 27).

April 3, 7:00 A.M.

Capitalism's greatest predicament is that several paradoxes of the human condition combine to turn capitalist successes into failures.

Take affluence: Capitalism is the only system that can create abundance. The non-capitalist world, no matter how rich in natural resources, has been and is likely to remain a world of scarcity. But it turns out that affluence is straining capitalist society to the breaking point. We were not prepared for the disintegration of values and the weakening of social discipline caused by the elimination of scarcity.

Take efficiency: Capitalist production is the most efficient the world has seen. It takes fewer workers to do a job in a capitalist society than anywhere else. But, by using as few workers as possible, capitalist society is without the wide diffusion of a sense of usefulness essential for social stability. So far, capitalism has not known how to cope with chronic unemployment.

Take change: Capitalist society is the most open to change. It is the only truly revolutionary society. The self-styled revolutionaries once in power prize stability above everything else, and the societies they dominate become economically and culturally stagnant. However, as change accelerates, capitalist societies are finding themselves in deep trouble. They are discovering that even the most desirable changes are upsetting traditions, customs and routines—all the arrangements which make everyday life predictable. And there is no telling how long a society that cannot take things for granted—a society with few axioms—can keep on an even keel.

Take mass education: It was the capitalists and not the intellectuals who initiated and promoted mass education. In capitalist America every mother's son can go to college. Most capitalist societies are being swamped with educated people who disdain the triviality and hustle of the marketplace and pray for a new social order that will enable them to live meaningful, weighty lives. The education explosion is now a more immediate threat to capitalist societies than a population explosion.

April 4, 6:40 A.M.

It is difficult to remember what a godsend the Second World War was to millions of Americans. Not only did the war finally end the Great Depression but the sudden need for workers opened the gates of exclusive unions to all comers. Prices were stable and it was easy to save money. Many who achieved some excellence in recent decades had their first chance during the war.

Small tightly knit circles are a peculiarity of creative milieus. You find them in Periclean Athens, in Renaissance Florence and Antwerp, and in Paris and late Hapsburg Vienna. Emulation, example, praise and assistance are at their best in such circles. Nevertheless, I shudder when I imagine what my life would have been as a member of such a circle. I always wanted to be left alone—not to have anyone to vie with, and not to have an example.

April 5, 9:45 A.M.

Taking too much for granted cuts people off from reality. The generation that stumbled into the First World War took civilization for granted. There was nowhere an awareness that a civilized pattern of life is almost as easily marred as the markings on butterfly wings. Yet we are also finding out that without axioms there is no social stability or continuity—that without taking things for granted there can be no civilized living.

How good I feel when I do my duty! I ought to invent a whole chain of duties and revel in their performance. Is not this the way the pious live full lives?

April 6, 4:00 A.M.

A painful twist of the left arm woke me up. I do not feel sleepy.

I try to imagine what Prime Minister Rabin said to Secretary of State Kissinger at their last parting. America's abandonment of Vietnam was in the air. "You are an American Secretary of State, and the interests of America should be uppermost in your mind. You are also a Jew whose relatives died in gas chambers while the whole civilized world looked on and did not lift a finger. The destruction of Israel would not affect America more adversely than did the fall of South Vietnam. Can we accept a condition in which our survival would depend on America's good will and good faith? Would you accept such a condition were you the Prime Minister of Israel, which you might have become had your parents gone to Israel instead of the United States?"

It does not make sense for a non-Israeli, however knowledgeable, sensitive and benevolent, to tell Israel what to do in order to survive. Israel is the foremost authority on national survival.

Do my dark thoughts reflect the weariness of a troubled old man rather than objective situations? Do I give voice to personal weariness when I maintain that this country cannot go on indefinitely as it has done in the past—the same squirrel cage, the same ups and downs? I am convinced that we have to stop running, stop wanting what we no longer really want.

April 7, 8:10 A.M.

Everything seemed to make sense in the nineteenth century: Industrialization, railways, steamships, explorations, empire building. America in particular was up to its neck in the purposeful action of taming a continent. Even the bloodiest Civil War made sense since it was fought to preserve one nation indivisible.

I have long assumed that the stagnation of the Arab world is due to the congeniality of the religion of Islam—its lack of the inner contradictions and tensions which stretch souls. But it seems that hashish is also a factor. The Mongol invasion in the thirteenth century which put an end to Arab supremacy also introduced hashish. Egyptian doctors have blamed this drug for the sluggishness of Egyptian workers. Will the use of marijuana have a similar effect on American workers?

The tendency has been to see Americans' phenomenal conformity as a curse. Actually, the fact that we can be shaped by example more readily than other people is an advantage in a world that for some mysterious reason cannot produce great leaders. In this country, impressive acts of courage and dedication staged by relatively small groups will find millions of emulators. Such groups can do for us many of the things we expect from an outstanding leader.

April 8, 7:00 A.M.
      I have drawn from the public library two books by Hans Kohn. I am interested in the process by which the rational, hopeful, peaceful, stable nineteenth century gave rise to the absurd, bloodsoaked, unstable twentieth century. It could be of course that there was no process but only an accidental, fateful stupidity—the First World War.

What would have happened had Hitler not been pathologically anti-Jewish? If after he had come to power Hitler had allowed Jews to continue their work in industry and science, they might have given him the atomic bomb. Anyhow, a benevolent attitude toward the Jews would probably have enabled Hitler to come to terms with Britain and France and thus have a free hand in Eastern Europe. He might even have made use of Jews as negotiators with the free world.

We can never love as totally as we hate. Hitler hated the Jews more than he loved Germany, more than he loved power, and more than he loved victory.

April 9, 7:50 A.M.

Reading Hans Kohn about his youth, I am aware how hard it is for an educated young man to develop his own thoughts and shape his own attitudes. At his age I was on the run. I was not immersed in the spirit of an age. I lived in a timeless world.

One need not be profound to predict the future. On the contrary, the seed of the future is on the surface of the present and is not seen by those who look for hidden truths. During the first miners' strike in 1910 the near-sighted Sir Edward Grey, by magnifying what he saw, predicted that trade unions would ultimately supplant parliament. It is true that in this case a naïve view of history aided prediction. Sir Edward saw a chain of displacements reaching back into the past: the barons displaced the crown, the middle class displaced the barons, and the workers were destined to displace the middle class and its parliament.

Have the young and the old exchanged roles? It is the young now who are pious, austere, enamored of old fashions, and sexually more experienced.

Hans Kohn underlines the fact that the four years of the First World War were a deeper break in history than the twenty-five years of war set off by the French Revolution. Still, it is true that the stupid First World War would not have been there to stumble into had it not been for the rabid chauvinism which infected every soul; and this chauvinism was brewed in the second half of the nineteenth century.

Western nationalism declined after the First World War. Hitler revived it in Germany in the 1930s, and the Second World War breathed life onto it elsewhere. But the decline continued after the war. It is curious that Kohn, a knowledgeable historian, did not foresee the pacific, pro-Western temper of postwar Germany. There was a widespread assumption that Germany would remain what it was.

It is my impression that only during the past hundred years have the aftermaths of wars been more fateful than the wars. Through most of history the momentous events preceded or took place during wars. The classic example is of the French Revolution preceding the revolutionary and Napoleonic wars. But since 1870 the fateful events have come after the wars: the birth of a United Germany after the Franco-Prussian war, the Bolshevik and Nazi revolutions after the First World War, Russian hegemony and the rebirth of China after the Second World War. It is significant that, with the exception of Churchill, the outstanding leaders of our time came to the fore not during but after wars. This was true of Lenin, Stalin, Hitler, Adenauer, de Gaulle and Mao.

April 10, 9:30 A.M.

The nineteenth century was dominated by men of action. The men of words just talked: they philosophized, theorized, prophesied and schemed extravagantly and recklessly because they knew that their words would not lead to action (January 5).

The twentieth century became a century of words par excellence. It not only saw the extravagant words of the nineteenth century become flesh but in no other century have so many men of words become spectacular men of action. In no other century have words been so dangerous. Yet few have recognized this fact. The free world refused to take Hitler's words seriously and at present hardly anyone outside Israel is alarmed by wild Arab talk about eliminating the Jewish state.

Hans Kohn's *Living in a World Revolution* was written in the early 1960s. It is good about Europe before the First World War but anemic about contemporary affairs and the recent past. There is no mention of the world's indifference to the fate of the Jews under Hitler. He includes Lenin among "the great emancipators of modern times."

I have a hunch that I might find more on the passage from the nineteenth to the twentieth century in Laqueur's book on Zionism than in Hans Kohn's *Political Ideologies of the Twentieth Century*. Herzl, the founder of Zionism, was one of the few people who sensed the coming of a holocaust. He knew that the civilized Occident was threatened by a wave of barbarism. It is of interest that, whereas in the closing days of the nineteenth century there were Jews who were straining their ears for the first crack of doom, thirty years later few of them believed in the coming of the Hitlerian apocalypse.

April 11, 7:50 A.M.

Backward countries are crying about the maldistribution of the world's wealth: one quarter of the world's population has three quarters of the wealth. Not a word is said about how wealth comes into being; the toil, sweat and self-denial which make an accumulation of wealth possible. This is how a once poor and backward Japan became an affluent country. It is curious how in both domestic and international affairs there is at present a stubborn refusal to see a connection between effort and income. It is widely assumed that individuals or countries are poor because they are exploited or discriminated against.

Hebrew fanaticism was born during the Babylonian captivity and became full-blown when the fascination with Hellenism threatened Jewish uniqueness. Fanaticism was the invention of a small, weak national entity fighting for survival. It became a scourge when appropriated by large, powerful bodies— churches, states, parties—in a struggle for supremacy. The unexampled success of organizations armed with fanaticism has led clear-sighted thinkers like Renan and Keynes to believe that "Only fanatics can found anything," that "The future lies in the hands of those who are not undeceived," and that "An age can only be great if it is bred up in believing what is preposterous."

100

Yet the Greeks achieved greatness without a belief in "vital lies."

April 12, 10:30 A.M.

Since communist countries are not equally inefficient, one ought not to blame communism for Russia's incredible inefficiency in the mechanics of everyday life. Repairing a car in Russia is a nightmare of negligence, ignorance, chicanery, theft and general bungling. There is evidence that things are different in Rumania, Hungary and several other communist countries. One is justified, therefore, in blaming the Russians rather than their system for the mess.

However, judging by the wonders performed by Russian peasants on their tiny private plots of land, there is reason to believe that a machine shop run by Russians as a private undertaking would be as efficient as any in the world. The present inefficiency should be attributed, therefore, to a Russian inaptitude for communism. Communism does not work in Russia. It works in China, Vietnam, Mongolia and some other countries. The Russians have a singular aptitude for private enterprise.

I remember how startled I was when old Mrs. C. told me that psychoanalysis is a chief destroyer of authority. Her words came from a deep, dark well of experience. It is strange that Vienna, the capital of a decaying Hapsburg empire, should have contributed so greatly to the decline of the Occident. It produced both Freud and Hitler.

April 13, 7:30 A.M.

There were anarchic intervals in the history of most countries: "In those days there was no king in Israel: every man did that which was right in his own eyes." We are told how unprecedentedly new our time is, but our troubles and difficulties are not new. There is nothing new in the decay of communities, the crumbling of authority, and the defiance of the young.

101

In an authoritarian regime it looks as if despotic power has usurped the authority of family, church, unions and so on. Actually, it was the decay of traditional authority that prepared the ground for dictatorship. Those who try to weaken established authority in order to enlarge individual freedom unknowingly clear the way for the coming of tyranny.

Everyone counts and no one weighs. If a white man in Africa has more enterprise than a hundred blacks, then Rhodesia has a white population of 27 million rather than 270,000. Israel holds its own in the Arab world because an Israeli weighs more than an Arab. It is a symptom of the Occident's underestimation of its strength that so many are panicked by the prospect of a confrontation with the backward two-thirds of the world.

April 19, 8:45 A.M.

I have spent several days on the final draft of the new book. It will be a slighter book than I thought—little over a hundred printed pages. I threw out several strident chapters. I no longer want to bark. But I hang on to my prejudices. They are the testicles of my mind.

April 20, 7:00 A.M.

In his autobiography John Nef says of the philosopher George Mead that "One thing that kept him from publishing as a philosopher was a strong belief that anything he wrote would no longer be true by the time it got into print." This suggests that contemporary philosophy is a fad that sooner or later goes out of date. The strange thing is that at present books based on facts rather than philosophical speculation are often overtaken by a similar fate. Facts have become as perishable as opinions. This holds true even of scientific facts. Only the human condition has remained timeless.

It has been often said that writers and artists compensate themselves for what they have missed in the realm of imposing action. But the reverse is even more true. Many outstanding men of action have been frustrated writers and artists. Failed dramatists in particular probably have a weakness and a talent for history making. Theodor Herzl, who wanted more than anything else to become a great playwright and did not succeed, staged the drama of political Zionism. Here is an entry in his diary (June 10, 1895): "Come to think of it I am still a dramatist. I picked poor people in rags off the street, put gorgeous costumes on them, and have them perform for the world a wonderful pageantry of my composition."

April 21, 8:50 A.M.

The British had it easy in the nineteenth century. They were ahead of everybody in industry and commerce, and their fleet made them invincible. They came to see their paramountcy as natural rather than something that had to be kept up by effort. They were not shaken out of their complacency even when eager-beaver Germans began to breathe down their necks.

Actually, the British tendency to take things for granted was typical of the nineteenth century; what that century did not know proved more fateful than what it knew.

At present, to be practical is to expect the worse.

It is noteworthy that Islam, a religion of the sword, made headway among the defeated in Asia and Africa while Christianity, a religion of meekness, was embraced and propagated by the warrior tribes of Europe but made little headway among the meek.

Machines may make people superfluous, but they cannot make them harmless. No matter how many and how ingenious the machines there will always be people around to mess things up.

I am more than ever convinced that the intellectual's hopes and fears are not shared by the majority of common people. The dismay which darkens our spirits has nothing to do with the sins of government or with the threats to human survival such as population explosion, pollution or a nuclear holocaust. No, our dark mood stems from the inability of parents to protect their children against pitfalls and snares, and from the inflation which puts to nought our efforts to provide for a rainy day.

The Chinese are the only ideologists who are good psychologists.

Lenin sprung a leak in the cesspool of Russian history and the stench has poisoned the civilized world.

In human affairs the immaterial is more weighty than anything that can be weighed and measured. The unpredictability of man has its source in the interaction between the fictitious and the real. The purely fictitious and the purely real are usually predictable.

April 22, 6:00 A.M.
    I am still looking for a wholly new train of thought. Actually, at my age, the mind is better elaborating and deepening the familiar than groping for a new beginning. I find I have my own key for any problem that is brought up. Thus, although I keep looking for something totally new, there is the conviction in the back of my mind that there is nothing new under the sun.

The early Greek philosophers were fantastic creatures. They were immersed in revelations and visions. "A light," said Kant, "broke on the first man who demonstrated the properties of the isosceles triangle." The world was a fabulous goldfield—

the meanest fact had in it nuggets of ideas. They expected the unexpected and found it. And there was not an idea they could not express in a sentence or two; and what they wrote sounded like inspired oracles.

After all that we have seen with our own eyes there ought not to be a grownup person who is not contemptuous of the gibberish about an ideal society and does not look for the lineaments of a commissar in the features of an idealist loudmouth.

The trouble is that the young who nowadays want to make history are not interested in history. They are unbelievably ignorant of much that has happened in this terrible century. They will follow anyone who wants to clear the ground for a new world by sweeping away all that exists.

April 23, 7:45 A.M.
        The British are returning to paradise without fanfare and shouts of triumph. They have revoked, in a whisper, the ukase that with the sweat of his brow man shall eat bread. It will be a subdued paradise on a manicured little island. Could it become a prison?

Societies can be vigorous without being free, truthful, noble, etc. A society decays not when it loses esthetic, intellectual or moral excellence but when its character becomes enfeebled—when its people are without courage, self-discipline and enterprise.

April 24, 10:00 A.M.
        I am reading a book about the Zulus. Shaka, the founder of the Zulu nation, reminds me of Stalin. He used terror to induce malleability. The knowledge that at any moment one might be liquidated at the whim of a leader is a powerful agency for turning people into malleable clay. Shaka kept up daily

executions. His power over his people was such that he could impose sexual abstinence on his warriors.

The question is: How did Shaka and Stalin impose their will on a band of henchmen who did the liquidating unquestioningly? The acquisition and exercise of absolute power is a dark matter. Both Shaka and Stalin had the implacability of a force of nature.

The Zulu nation created by Shaka lasted about fifty years. Another nation in that part of the world, the Metabelle, also had a short life span. Up to now the Occident has not known anything like Shaka's sudden, powerful, shortlived creation. Hitler's Third Reich was the nearest thing.

April 25, 7:30 A.M.

I ought to have a good chapter on hope in the new book. The role hope plays in the life of a modern society is so taken for granted that we are unaware of its novelty. Through most of history mankind lived without the vision of a shining future around the corner. The conviction prevailed that successive generations and ages would be "as alike as drops of water." The belief that the future will be better and happier than the past was introduced by the French Encyclopedists and preached by the French revolutionaries. "Happiness," said Saint Just, "is a new idea in Europe." America's birth almost coincided with the birth of this climate of hope.

Hope is at present a vital social ingredient. It is indispensable not only in the maintenance of social vigor but in the preservation of social cohesion and discipline. And nowhere in the modern world has hope been so central and natural as in America. The taming of a savage continent in an incredibly short time was powered by boundless hope. As recently as the 1950s Americans still felt themselves in the van, pioneering the future. Yet by 1970 a British correspondent in Washington could pontificate without being challenged that if America is the future, the future does not work.

Who slew America's hope? We were all there—workingmen,

businessmen, politicians, soldiers, old and young, rich and poor, learned and ignorant. But the murder weapon was forged in the radical-chic salons of Manhattan and Washington, and in the word factories of our foremost universities.

April 26, 7:45 A.M.

The ancient Hebrews were precursors not only of the Occident (March 18) but of the modern age of hope. Usually, when we speak of the uniqueness of the ancient Hebrews, we have in mind their worship of one, invisible God. Actually, Hebrew monotheism went hand in hand with two other unique manifestations. The Hebrews were the first optimists. Alone among the peoples of antiquity they located a golden age not in the past but in the future. Their *tikva,* hope, envisioned a glorious future for humanity on this earth. (The Old Testament makes no mention of a heavenly kingdom. All of God's promises were to be fulfilled here on earth.)

Curiously, this faith in the future was joined with a passionate preoccupation with the past. The ancient Hebrews made history rather than cosmic events the meaningful drama of the universe. Their rites and celebrations concerned themselves not with the cycle of the seasons but with historical events.

It is my feeling that there is an interconnection between faith in one, invisible God and a vivid awareness of future and past. People without hope need tangible idols to worship. It is only when we hope "for what we see not" that we can believe in what we see not. So, too, the making of historical rather than natural events the central drama of the universe was part of the downgrading of nature which made possible the belief in a God who was not part but the creator of nature. There can be no monotheistic faith without a belief in the uniqueness and primacy of man. The one God who created nature made man his viceroy on earth.

Strangely, a modern Occident that functions largely without faith in God has embraced the Hebrew *tikva* and the passionate preoccupation with the past.

April 27, 8:00 A.M.

The tragedy of the second half of the nineteenth century was the failure of German statesmanship to see Russia as a deadly threat (January 6). Bismarck would easily rank as Europe's foremost statesman had he recognized that the task of a United Germany was to push the Russian slave empire back to the Urals and have a free western Russia integrated with Europe. It was the crowning absurdity of an absurd twentieth century that a unified Germany set off two World Wars which ruined the Occident and brought the Russian slave empire to the bank of the Elbe.

I said it was a failure of German statesmanship. Actually, the failure was European.

Listening to Mozart, I can see how much Beethoven borrowed from him. Did I not know that it is Mozart I am hearing, I would think that the music is that of an imitator of Beethoven who didn't quite make the grade.

April 28, 7:50 A.M.

We usually think of youth as an age of hope. Actually, the young are immersed in the present and their hopes are so immediate as to be indistinguishable from desire. On the other hand, to the old hope is a tonic that stimulates digestion and blood circulation and makes sleep more restful. The old are stretched by expecting something around the corner.

The danger inherent in reform is that the cure may be worse than the disease. Reform is an operation on the social body; but unlike medical surgeons reformers are not on guard against unpredictable side effects which may divert the course of reform toward unwanted results. Moreover, quite often the social doctors become part of the disease.

108

I have suggested (April 12) that Russia is in chronic trouble because of the incompatibility between Russian nature and communism. Yet it is by no means self-evident that an incompatibility between a doctrine and those who adopt it unavoidably spells trouble.

One cannot think of a more profound incompatibility than that between the Christian doctrine of meekness and Europe's warrior tribes who embraced it (February 5); yet this contradiction generated a tension which made Europe the most dynamic part of the world. Why, then, does the contradiction in Russia result in stagnation? The answer probably is that, whereas the warrior tribes fervently believed in a Christianity that went against their grain, the Russians do not believe in communism. There is no pull between opposites which would stretch souls.

April 29, 8:00 A.M.

Eighteenth-century Britain has for me a special fascination. Its people displayed a Dostoevskian eccentricity. The upper crust intercopulated so that it was impossible to sort the children out. They were one family. What amazes me is their power of words. Both men and women wrote powerful prose. The chaotic spelling makes it seem as if they were inventing the language as they wrote.

I have never had absolute command of language. Words have always been to me accidental, unnatural, uninevitable. I have spent my life trying to master words, but they never became part of me. I always have to search for them, pull them in by the neck. I use as few of them as I can.

Several years ago, I gave the University of California at Berkeley a sum of money that would yield at least five hundred dollars a year to be given as a prize for an essay of five hundred words. A dollar a word! There was an outcry from students and some of the faculty: "What can one say in five hundred words?" My answer was that there is not an idea that cannot be expressed in two hundred words, and the prize allows words enough for two and a half original ideas.

The director of the Slavic-Soviet center at Pennsylvania State University went to Peking in 1974 and told his hosts that America had warned the Russians not to start a war with China. I doubt whether he knew what he was talking about and whether the Chinese believed him. America has no interest in preventing Russia from starting a war with China. If we could do it we would push the Russians into China and make sure they got tangled up in an endless war. This, as I have suggested (April 8), is one way of solving the Russian problem.

In the same journal (*The Journal of General Education,* 1974, vol. XXVI, no. 3) Thomas Varlick, who also visited China, makes the startling statement that China's feat of feeding and clothing nine hundred million people would not have been possible "without a particular mental set which simply cannot coexist with modern, basic scientific inquiry." Mao had to convince hundreds of millions of manual workers that the entire destiny of the country hung upon what every one of them was doing. He had to extol manual labor above mental labor and generate hostility toward purely intellectual accomplishments. In such a climate basic science cannot thrive.

April 30, 8:00 A.M.

As long as a society has an enclave of legitimate recklessness, spoiling children need not have fatal consequences. In the heyday of Britain's aristocracy, Lord Holland could propound the doctrine that "the young are always right," and indulge his son Charles when he smashed a gold watch, saying: "If you must, you must." This Charles grew up to be a reckless gambler and womanizer but also a brilliant, daring political figure—an aristocrat who toasted "Our Sovereign the People."

In this country, business is the main enclave of recklessness and it is my hunch that spoiled children have the makings of daring business operators. It was disastrous that in the 1960s the spoiled children of the rich turned their backs on business and vented their recklessness on campuses.

What is it that shapes a face? There are nonentities who look distinguished. Many have remarked on the plainness of Lenin, Stalin and Hitler. They did not look like great men. It is of interest that Matthew Arnold made a similar remark about Lincoln. He praised Lincoln's virtues but added: "He had no distinction." And no one looked more common than Ulysses Grant: "An ordinary, scrubby-looking man with a slightly seedy look, as if he was out of office on half pay."

May 1, 7:00 A.M.
        In several Latin American countries the rich stash their money in foreign banks and dream of a life of bliss in Paris. They have a colonialist attitude toward their country. The mass of people are kept inert, ill-fed and ill-housed. Moreover, the children of the rich play at revolution during adolescence. Thus, in addition to the perpetuation of poverty, the rich contribute to political anarchy.

It is incredible how much pampering and bribing it needs to induce the rich to get richer. They call the bribes incentives. Clearly, it is assumed that it is the rich who keep the wheels turning. They not only avoid paying adequate taxes but are paid not to raise wheat and not to pump oil.

Despite space exploration and unprecedented discoveries in science and technology, the spirit of our age expresses itself more clearly in failures than in achievements. Our age is documented by fears rather than hopes.

        6:30 P.M.   I am reading the autobiography of Duff Cooper, *Old Men Forget*. It gives me more pleasure than I have had for some time. He wanted the best of everything and with effort and luck managed to have it. All his close friends were killed in the First World War. He survived although he was in the thick of battle and was mentioned in dispatches. You realize what a hemorrhage of England's finest blood that war was.

May 2, 7:45 A.M.

Contrary to what one would expect, it is the more ancient civilizations that can assimilate borrowings from others without ill effects. The more distinct and unassailable the identity of a society the more easily and safely it can imitate foreign models. Japan's copious borrowings from China did not make it less uniquely Japanese. The same is true of Japan's borrowings from the Occident. China too did not become less Chinese by adopting communism and has not sickened on what it borrowed.

Perhaps, under ideal conditions, communism might be compatible with individual freedom and even with abundance. What are the ideal conditions? A fairly advanced country with a disciplined, energetic and highly skilled population that has wearied of competition and the lust for possessions. The aim of such a society would be an unhurried, culturally rich existence. Whatever it had of abundance would be an accidental bonus.

It never ceases to delight me when I come across a statement about the great antiquity of art—that man painted pictures before he made useful utensils. It gives me pleasure to think that man began his career on this globe as an artist. We are prepared for the unexpected when we are told that a certain statesman, businessman, scientist or scholar started out as an artist.

May 3, 8:30 A.M.

You would think that when a man has something worthwhile to say his chief concern would be to make himself understood and he would write as simply as he could. But it is not so. There are not above a score of scholars in this country at present who express themselves in lucid prose.

In Britain good writing has a long tradition, and it is practiced by scientists and scholars. Lord Rutherford used to say that he was not sure an idea had merit until he could express it in ordinary language understood by charwomen.

The French have long been masters of lucid writing. French thinkers from Descartes on believed that there is not an idea that cannot be expressed in language intelligible to everybody. In the eighteenth century Rivarol maintained that that which is not lucid is not French. Of late, however, French writers have become enamored of existentialist, Marxist and Hegelian double talk. It is the British who now write English the way the French used to write French.

Hegel's great victory in the twentieth century has been to make Frenchmen write like Germans. Actually, it was Hitler who made Frenchmen receptive to Hegel. They needed fig leaves of obscurantism to cover the shame of the German occupation.

In 1953 Duff Cooper was convinced that de Gaulle was finished. "The curious ineptitude for happiness has proved an unfortunate quality in the character of a remarkable man, and has contributed to the failure of his career." In *The True Believer,* written in the late 1940s, I predicted a great career for de Gaulle. I based my prediction on de Gaulle's capacity to win and hold the allegiance of a band of outstanding lieutenants. Most leaders who fail lack this capacity. Trotsky is a classic example.

What is it that enables a leader to evoke loyalty? Certainly most of the leaders who had this ability were not themselves loyal.

I cannot think of a national goal so legitimate and realizable as the determination to use the unemployed young and blacks who pack the cities in a concerted undertaking to rehabilitate the continent and clean up and reconstruct the decaying cities. It is not beyond our reach to have by the end of the century cities without ghettos, with safe streets, with spacious squares and parks, and a continent unpolluted and replenished.

Britain has any number of brilliant economists, and the labor government is receptive to their advice, yet the economic situation in Britain is dismal and getting worse. A reporter in the *Guardian Weekly* says that the economists who are pulling the delicate levers of the economy do not know what the impact of what they do will be on jobs, prices and the balance of payments. Still, the economists go on advising and teaching, and some are given Nobel Prizes. Right now there is no reason to believe that social scientists have a special competence to counsel, guide and predict. Yet the universities keep on producing them and governments keep on employing them.

It is incredible that as recently as the 1950s the British were unaware of what fate had in store for them. Years have now the weight of centuries. It is to their credit that the British know how to decline gracefully. The French have messed up Europe for a century in their refusal to adjust themselves to the reality of being a second-class country.

May 4, 6:30 A.M.

I woke up this morning thinking about old King David. I reread the opening paragraph of the first book of Kings: "Now King David was old and they covered him with clothes but he could not get warm. Therefore his servants said unto him: 'Let a young maiden be sought for my lord, a young virgin, let her wait upon the king, let her cherish him, let her lie in thy bosom, that my lord may be warm.' So they sought for a beautiful maiden throughout the land of Israel and found Abishag the Shunamite and brought her to the king. The maiden was very beautiful, and she cherished the king and ministered to him, but the king knew her not." Has anyone painted David with the Shunamite maiden? David's leathery, worn face, the lost look in his brooding eyes, the white hair on his skeletal chest. I cannot see the maiden.

With its boundless hope and unimpaired authority the nineteenth century could view human affairs as rational and predictable. The human condition was seen as something unclean and was not allowed to rise to the surface and foul up the flow of events.

Things changed after the First World War. With the loss of hope and the breakdown of authority, the logic of events came to the fore and life became subject to the irrationality, unpredictability and primitiveness of the human condition. Words acquired magical power (April 10), and medicine men and tribal chieftains shaped events.

It is probably extremely rare for a person to feel, even for a brief moment, that what he is and does are absolutely fitting and cannot be bettered. And it is a gift from heaven for an older person to have such a moment.

May 5, 9:45 A.M.

I suspect that American obscurantist writing has German roots. German universities were the nursery of American scholarship during the nineteenth century. The Germans disdain lucidity as superficial. The least-understood philosophers have among them the greatest authority. It has been argued that the inability of the Germans to develop lucid prose has been one of the disasters of European civilization.

Strangely, two great Germans—Frederick the Great and Charles the Fifth—thought that German was good only for talking to horses.

American articles are usually longer and American books thicker than their British counterparts. When I go through a shelf of books on a subject I begin with the thin volumes. Now and then I find a thin and a thick book by the same author on the same subject. Usually, the thin book is of an earlier date; and it often turns out that in the thin book the author reveals what he knows and in the thick book he tries to conceal what he does not know.

Good historians are an exception. They may produce a thin volume toward the end of their days summarizing their ideas, and it is a treat to read them.

About David and the Shunamite maiden: "The lost look in brooding eyes" is wrong. Rather eyes like live coals glowing in a shriveled face, and the hair on his head standing on end. The maiden at his side is excited, with twinkling, mischievous eyes. Two playmates.

May 6, 8:00 A.M.

A nation is on its way out when it devotes much of its wealth and energies to the care and welfare of the least-endowed segment of its population and puts a low ceiling on the rewards of those who ceaselessly strive and achieve.

It is becoming increasingly difficult for haves and have-nots to live together in one society. As never before, it is clear that a massive attempt to end poverty must in various ways discomfort the haves, while under conditions optimal for the haves the disillusionment of the have-nots threatens social stability.

The hopeful nineteenth century took it for granted that the march of progress would turn have-nots into haves. The Bolsheviks tried to solve the problem by turning haves into have-nots. But in the last third of the twentieth century we have seen it demonstrated that money, education and armies of dedicated social workers cannot cure chronic poverty. We also know that turning haves into have-nots results in social decline and stagnation. The only alternative left is separation—to have two different societies side by side (March 3). In one society the chronically poor will have ideal opportunities to learn new skills and become self-reliant. In the other society the haves will be free to wheel and deal, compete, run risks, build and tear down, experiment—in short, do as they please.

       7:45 P.M.   Finished the biography of Admiral Spruance by T. B. Buell. The book held my attention though the writing is undistinguished and the events described familiar. The practical, unmomentous style of American leadership has for me a special fascination. It is particularly striking in the armed forces, which are basically aristocratic. A total absence of rhetoric; an unflustered, undramatic style of history making; a readiness to delegate power; and, finally, an enormous capacity to learn from events.

May 7, 7:50 A.M.
       I doubt whether any book or film could do justice to the battle of Midway. The Americans did not fight for a fatherland or a holy cause. There was a job to do and they did it. They were not only outnumbered by the Japanese but also outclassed. The Japanese Zero fighter could outclimb, outrun and outmaneuver any plane the Americans had. The American fliers were inferior in battle experience and in morale. There was nothing on the American side to match the fanatical dedication of Japanese fighting men. The Japanese had every reason to believe that taking Midway would be "as easy as twisting a baby's arm."
The American planes came in clumsily, doggedly and recklessly. A large number of them were blown out of the sky, and most of their bombs missed the target. But they kept coming, and eventually sank all the Japanese carriers with all their planes, and most of their irreplaceable veteran crews. It was a fateful victory and a turning point in the war. Yet, throughout the battle, all that the American commanders, from Admiral Nimitz down, could tell their men was "There is a job to do."

During the Civil War, educated people in Europe took it for granted that America's days were numbered and they were on the whole glad of it. It is startling to read what the enlightened Walter Bagehot had to say on the subject *(Historical Essays):* "Europe at large and England especially have not grieved much at the close proximity of America's fall, but perhaps rejoiced at the prospect of some marked change from a policy . . . of which the events were mean, the actors base, and the working inexplicable. A low vulgarity has deeply displeased the cultivated mind of Europe, and the American Union will fall little regretted even by those whose race is akin, whose language is identical, whose weighted opinions are on most subjects the same as theirs. The unpleasantness of mob government has never before been exemplified so conspicuously, for it never before has worked on so large a scene."

It needs an effort to realize how offended Europe's cultivated, aristocratic minds were by the spectacle of common people eloping with history to a vast, new continent and essaying to do there all the things—build cities, found states, lead armies—which from the beginning of time were reserved for the privileged orders.

May 8, 6:40 A.M.

In any consideration of creative milieus Hungary of 1867–1914 should occupy a prominent place. The Hungarian aristocracy in its effort to hold up its end in the partnership with the Austro-Germans did all it could to stimulate the growth of Hungarian culture. There was a massive, methodical effort to realize creative potentialities. The spotting and encouragement of talent in the Budapest of that period were as effective as they were in Renaissance Florence. Most of the fabulous Hungarians who made their mark in Europe and America had their start in this creative milieu. If I remember correctly, they were all graduates of the same famous high school.

When Wycliffe translated the Bible from the Latin into "the tongue of the Angels," he was excoriated by his betters for scattering the evangelical pearls "to be trampled by the swine."

The educated have equated common people with swine almost from the invention of writing. It is curious that in Russia, despite the official glorification of the masses, there is an intense loathing of common people among the intellectuals. In this country in the 1960s the SDS semester-intellectuals spoke of the majority as "honkey swine."

May 9, 8:00 A.M.

Renan was probably the only historian in the rational nineteenth century who was obsessed with the paradoxes of the human condition (May 4). It is no wonder that his contemporaries dismissed his insights as too farfetched and did not take him seriously as a historian.

Renan became wonderfully timely after the First World War. His seldom read *History of the People of Israel* (in five volumes) sheds more light on the bewildering events of the Stalin-Hitler decades than do the findings of the most expert observers, be they scholars or statesmen.

When we read what some revolutionary intellectuals wrote about the evils of the nineteenth century we are startled by how closely their words fit the realities of twentieth-century Russia. Here is Alexander Herzen's description of Western Europe in the middle of the nineteenth century: "A secular inquisition reigns supreme, civil rights have been suspended. . . . There is only one moral force that still has authority over men . . . and that is fear which is universal."

The revolutionaries made of history what Engels said it was: "the most terrible of divinities driving its triumphant chariot over piles of cadavers." It is the rage of the intellectuals that has ravaged the twentieth century.

9:00 P.M.   I spent four hours in the park walking leisurely. The call of the quail reminded me of the great silence of the wilderness I knew in my gold-prospecting days. I am like a man with a heart condition who has not a thought on which death is not engraved.

119

May 10, 6:30 A.M.

The nineteenth century was naïve (February 23) because it did not know the end of the story. It did not know what happens when dedicated idealists come to power; it did not know the intimate linkage between idealists and policemen, between being your brother's keeper and being his jailkeeper.

It is disconcerting that present-day young who did not know Stalin and Hitler are displaying the old naïveté. After all that has happened they still do not know that you cannot build utopia without terror, and that before long terror is all that's left.

Some of the hands seen in cave paintings have a finger or the joint of a finger missing. The conclusion of the scholarly experts: "Mutilation; the sign of religious practices." It did not occur to these experts that hunting and the chipping of stone tools can be hard on fingers, at least as hard as longshoring. Missing fingers or joints of fingers are common on the waterfront.

How startling the admonition in the Bible not to favor a poor man in his quarrels—not to treat the poor more equal than equal.

May 11, 8:45 A.M.

Compared with man all living things are predictable automata. Man is unique in his unpredictability. To make man predictable is to dehumanize him. Yet, paradoxically, this uniquely unpredictable creature has to have a wholly predictable world around him in order to function well. He needs not only a predictable natural and social environment but also a predictable body and a more or less routinized everyday life.

Thus, throughout his existence man has been engaged in a passionate search for predictability. He uses whatever powers he has to turn variables into constants; and when his power is unchallenged he may turn his fellow men into predictable automata.

To maintain social discipline, an affluent society must know how to create a new kind of scarcity—a new category of vital needs that are not easily fulfilled. In an affluent society the vying and ceaseless striving which made material abundance possible will have to be directed toward new goals. Just as in a time of general scarcity societies had to implant and nurture the work ethic in order to survive, so in an era of general abundance they have to know how to induce a ceaseless striving for the realization of individual capacities and talents in order to preserve their stability and health. And by passing from an economy of matter to an economy of the spirit a society enters a world of incurable scarcity.

May 12, 6:30 A.M.

In a creative milieu the talented are not only encouraged and cultivated but are also left alone to stew in their own juice. This is something a communist regime cannot do. It both worships and fears the creative individual. It is convinced that the field of culture is also a seedbed of dissent and subversion, and needs constant weeding.

The British far left is doing all it can to accelerate inflation and unemployment. There is method in this madness. The far left intends to pick up the pieces when the economic system breaks down and build a truly socialist Britain. Can it succeed? The lethargy of the British workingman is by now so fixed that the revolutionaries will not have the human material to build with. Nowhere have revolutionary soul engineers known how to energize disenchanted workingmen. Indeed, at present, workingmen are more inert in socialist than in capitalist societies. The rebirth of a vigorous Britain will have to come some other way—perhaps through a violent reaction against the far

121

left. Chauvinism might well be the only means of raising British workers from their lethargy.

It is fascinating to see disparaged values become vital again. The readiness to work, which was expected to be of little value in an automated economy, is now recognized as an element of social vigor. Patriotism, debunked and decried, might be a decisive factor in the rehabilitation of Britain.

May 13, 8:10 A.M.

Von Karman's *The Wind and Beyond* is a delight. He is one of the prodigious Hungarians I have mentioned (May 8). I am learning something and also enjoying myself. Good stories. The one I like best is about David Helbert, the great mathematician. At a party in his house, his wife asked him to change his tie. He went up to the bedroom and did not return. When his wife went up to see what had happened to him she found him fast asleep in bed. He had taken off his tie, and since this was normally the first step in undressing he simply continued and went to sleep.

This delightful story reminded me of the predicament of the old: they have the failings and the needs of genius. They are as absent-minded as a great mathematician, and like creative people they need recognition and praise in order to function well.

Von Karman's father thought that the life span of an idea is 150 years (five generations). He predicted that nationalism, which took hold in 1800, would begin to die in 1950.

Of what do ideas die? Some die of excess. The excesses of the religious wars put an end to religiosity just as nationalist excesses are bringing nationalism to an end. Industrialism too seems likely to die of excess. The idea of hope died from expecting too much and taking too much for granted. The hopeful generation that stumbled into the First World War took civilized life for granted. The life span of the idea of hope, from the Encyclopedists to 1914, was about 150 years.

May 14, 7:30 A.M.

Social scientists dream of situations immune to interference by unpredictable human factors. But it turns out that in human affairs no situation is manproof. However high the degree of automation and however overpowering the non-human factors, the human elements of enterprise, courage, pride, faith, malice, stupidity, sloth and the capacity for mischief remain decisive.

Reading von Karman, one realizes what a potent key mathematics is for the unlocking of nature's secrets. One is also aware that, in aerodynamics as in man's soul, the trivial is not trivial. A slight change in design can have momentous consequences.

I love ideas as much as I love women. I derive a sensuous pleasure from playing with ideas. Genuine ideas dance and sing. They sparkle and twinkle with mirth and mischief. They titillate the mind, kindle the imagination, and warm the heart. They have grace and promise.

There is a homesickness for the Middle Ages in typical intellectuals. It was their golden age. Their superior status and social usefulness were unquestioned, and the masses knew their place. Thus when intellectuals come to power, they institute a new Middle Age, dominated by a secular church and a hierarchy of clerks, and served by a population of serfs cowed by doctrinaire doubletalk.

May 15, 7:00 A.M.

It seems that most historians are inclined to have a high opinion of active presidents. It may well be that history writers have a vested interest in history makers. Yet in the twentieth century active, do-good presidents have in one way or another contributed to the deterioration of the national character. The mess we are in now has its roots in the active presidencies of FDR, Truman, Kennedy and Johnson. It seems that every time an active president tried to solve a problem he created an insoluble problem. In retrospect, Eisenhower's ability to keep things from happening has almost an occult quality. I wonder what the course of events in the 1960s would have been had Kennedy and Johnson emulated Eisenhower rather than FDR.

Latin countries seem always politically on the brink. Non-Latin countries in Western Europe and North America have economic crises but are on the whole politically stable. It is of interest that Latin Quebec is introducing a brink into Canada's political life.

The greater political involvement of intellectuals in Latin countries may be a factor. The intellectuals are there at the center of the web of power. They not only organize political parties and shape public opinion but are often elected to high office. And there is clear evidence that intellectuals are too self-important and self-righteous to practice the give-and-take vital for the stability of a free society. Where there is no restraining power, intellectuals in politics are a divisive element with a natural bent for pullulating, zealous sects, cliques and factions. If an organization dominated by intellectuals is to keep stable it has to be authoritarian and intolerant of dissent. This is true of the Catholic church and of communist parties. De Gaulle, who sensed France's incompatibility with parliamentary democracy, did not go far enough in his innovations to ensure political stability. And it is quite fitting that the largest communist parties in Europe outside the Soviet orbit should be found in Latin countries.

May 16, 2:30 P.M.

Czarist Russia was an inefficient, backward and somewhat chaotic despotism. Its cultural life was dominated by a tyrannical censor. It was racked by violent dissent and police brutality. Yet, surprisingly, during the second half of the nineteenth century Czarist Russia produced writers, composers and scientists who rank with the greatest of our time. Clearly, despite its appalling drawbacks, Czarist Russia had the elements of a potent creative milieu. What were they?

There was an appreciative reading public that welcomed a good book as a national event. The publishing establishment celebrated and rewarded excellence. The censorship was inefficient. It compressed rather than repressed the creative drive. A paucity of opportunities for impressive action in business and politics allowed a copious flow of energies into cultural pursuits. There was a passion for discussion; talk was a national pastime. Finally, Russian society in the second half of the nineteenth century was subject to the pull of opposite poles, which stretched souls: national pride and self-contempt, hope and fear, worship of freedom and a slave mentality, a pull toward and a repulsion from Western Europe, a suspension between East and West and between barbarism and civilization.

About the capacity for prophesying. The Baltic barons, suspended between Germany and Russia, and with a foreign peasantry on their land, had both the inclination and the gift for prophesying. On the eve of the French Revolution, Baron Grimm wrote to Catherine of Russia: "Two empires will divide the world between them: Russia in the East, and America, which has gained its freedom in recent years, in the West; and we the people in between shall be too degraded to know what we have been." Thus when, about fifty years later, de Tocqueville prophesied the impending domination of the world by Russia and America, he was echoing something that was floating in the air.

9:00 P.M.   Though my life is meager, I have yet to meet a person with whom I would like to change places. I never wanted to be other than what I am. I have been wearing the same kind of clothes, cut my hair the same way, lived in the same style all my life.

Nor have I ever become disenchanted with America. I somehow always felt that I had no right to expect too much from this country. I know all the flaws and blemishes. But I also know that America was built largely by hordes of undesirables from Europe, and that had this country been populated by Europe's best and finest, we would now be in a worse mess.

May 17, 6:35 A.M.

In a post-industrial society it will become increasingly difficult to find work for everybody. How will the presence of millions of energetic, skilled workingmen rusting away in inaction affect social vigor?

A concerted effort to clean up the continent and renovate the large cities (May 3) might offer a temporary solution. But in the long run, post-industrial society will have to accept a drastic reduction of the work week to, say, twenty-four hours or less. This will involve a change in the role of work: rather than being the main content of life, work will be seen as a ritual and drill to maintain physical and mental health.

The distribution of goods was a problem of industrial societies which is now being solved. The problem of post-industrial society will be the distribution of work.

The bloodthirstiness of Marxist intellectuals is now being displayed in all its horror in Cambodia. The refugees who reach Thailand tell of mass slaughter, forced labor and starvation. The reporters who so lustily condemned the shortcomings of the anti-communist regimes in Cambodia and South Vietnam are now silent. There is no sign of journalistic venturesomeness to discover the truth. I can see the avalanche of reports by daring newspapermen had the atrocities been committed by a rightist rather than a Marxist Khmer Rouge.

May 18, 6:50 A.M.

I just finished *Akenfield, Portrait of an English Village,* by Ronald Blythe. It is a revealing book. The villagers whose words are recorded come from all walks of life. They are farmers, farm hands, craftsmen, housewives, a nurse, a teacher, a union organizer, a justice of the peace. These people are competent, intelligent and surprisingly articulate. They are not members of a decaying society. There seems to be no awareness in the countryside of the indolence and negligence in factories and mines which are turning Britain into a backward country.

It cheers me no end that Britain's fields are not neglected. Indeed, they are more productive and better cared for than they were at the turn of the century when Britain was in its imperial glory. Britain's industrial decline is probably irreversible. There is no reason to believe that British workingmen will change their present attitude toward work in the foreseeable future. Indolent workers and mediocre management will keep British industrial products non-competitive. It is also true that at least seventy-five percent of the population is urban. Still, with a vigorous countryside and a thriving cultural life social collapse cannot seem a real threat.

May 19, 10:30 A.M.

We must never get over the fact that one of the best-educated and most-advanced countries of the Occident became a willing instrument of Hitler's holocaust. Instead of repeating the clichés about the humanizing and civilizing effects of education we ought to think and speak about the dehumanizing effects of humiliation—how easily the bruised self sheds its humanity and its veneer of civilization. The humiliation of Germany by France after the First World War was a monumental blunder. It is to America's credit that it did not humiliate its defeated enemies after the Second World War. The humiliation of France during the Second World War will go on having pernicious consequences for decades.

A war is not won if the defeated enemy has not been turned into a friend. It should be easy for a conqueror to court the conquered. The injunction to love our enemy is easy to obey when it is a defeated enemy.

I cannot wholeheartedly condemn the Germans who followed Hitler. Who of us can know with certainty how he would have acted had he been a German living in Germany after the First World War? I am convinced that had Hitler not rejected the Jews so totally most of the German Jews would have been with him. Hitler was born of the humiliation that poisoned the souls of all Germans, both gentiles and Jews.

We refuse to accept it as self-evident that a democratic form of government is the most difficult to attain and maintain and that only few countries are fit for it. Without a strong middle class and a self-respecting working class democratic government is unworkable. Communist Russia could never become a democracy. And it is absurd to expect backward countries to become democratic overnight. These countries are not only without an adequate middle class and working force but most of them have a small but highly influential intellectual class that is authoritarian, and ill at ease in a parliamentary democracy (May 15).

May 20, 8:00 A.M.
In a communist country there is no pornography, no violence in the streets, no unemployment, no rat race, no corrupt welfare and poverty programs, and no ceaseless din of inane, brazen advertisements. Why, then, would I never choose to live in a communist country?

In a communist country the individual is never left alone. He is spied upon, bullied, forced to love what he hates, and paralyzed by fear and distrust. Above all, the savagely enforced prohibition of emigration makes it plain that a communist country is basically a prison. When you go to prison in a free country you escape pornography, unemployment, the rat race and so on. Yet no one chooses to go to prison to escape the evils of the outside world. We never hear of people trying to break into prison, and we shall never hear of people trying to steal into Russia the way thousands of Mexicans are risking their lives to enter America.

May 21, 7:00 A.M.
It is a general assumption that America became a great nation because of the abundance of its natural resources. The assumption is not shaken by the fact that Canada and Mexico did not become great despite their natural riches, and that a Japan that imports over ninety percent of its raw materials is catching up with the United States.

Whether Marxist or not, American historians are not hospitable to the idea that man makes history, that the human resources are more decisive than the natural—that courage, enterprise, skill and a passion for excellence are the ingredients of national vigor and greatness. Do they see doom around the corner now that our stores of oil and natural gas are running out, and other raw materials are nearing exhaustion?

Still, I wonder whether the vastness and riches of this continent were not a precondition for the formation of our unprecedented mass society in the second half of the nineteenth century. The masses who plunged into a virgin continent and tamed it in an incredibly short time were mindlessly wasteful. The fabulous natural riches gave them the time to become skilled men of action even as they wasted, so that eventually they could turn the ravaged land into a cornucopia of plenty.

11:00 P.M.   I spent almost two hours tracking a mistake in my bank book. The elation when I finally spotted the mistake is comical. I realized that since my retirement from the waterfront I have been without the frequent feeling of well being that comes from a job well done. Happiness comes from small things.

May 22, 9:15 A.M.
Coming of short-lived stock, I have felt most of my life that my days were numbered. Yet only now, at seventy-

three, do I have the feeling that there is no time left to make good what is lost or damaged—that any mistake I make is irremediable. Obviously, the sense of time is not purely a mental attitude but a function of the body.

What happens when a highly endowed person does not develop with his talents? It all depends on whether he has clear proof of his exceptional capacities. If he has, the unrealized talents will gnaw at his heart and mind. But, if a person is unaware of his talents, the buried gifts will give zest and sparkle to his everyday life.

The young in Western Germany seem more ruthlessly violent than the young in other democracies. It is probably a manifestation of the German passion for thoroughness, for doing a thing for its own sake. Hitler's final solution was an instance of German thoroughness in solving problems.

Intellectual extremism has blinded the Germans to the fact that truth is to be found not in absolutes but in nuances; hence their awkwardness in dealing with the paradoxes of the human condition. The Germans did not produce a Montaigne, Pascal or Francis Bacon. Could this be the reason why German literature did not reach a world audience (April 2)?

Everyday happenings are demonstrating before our eyes that without effective authority a free society tends toward anarchy. Loss of nerve at the center and excessive safeguards of individual liberty have made of freedom an evil that robs us of personal security, prevents the socialization of the young, destroys schools, breeds negligence in places of work, undermines morale in the armed forces, and turns the successes of a free society into failures. Libertarian legislators, judges, educators and doctrinaires will in retrospect be seen as the wreckers of free societies.

May 23, 6:00 A.M.

It is a tragic fact that the wound inflicted on Arab manhood by the emergence of a defiant Israel cannot be cured by reasonable solutions. There is the widespread conviction that the Arabs will become whole again only by wiping Israel off the face of the earth.

The present manufactures both past and future. A good book about the present should tell how past and future are made. It should throw a new light on the past, and provide niches into which future happenings will fit.

I am reading Yevgenia Ginzburg's *Journey into the Whirlwind.* She spent eighteen years in Stalin's camps. The Stalin-Hitler decades shaped my mind and I am still obsessed with the deliberate human degradation practiced by Russians and Germans on a vast scale. The passivity of the outside world during those terrible decades makes me scornful of the present fashionable agitation against all sorts of wrongs in non-communist countries. A world that did not raise its voice against the enormities of Stalin and Hitler is now crying out against injustice in Chile, Rhodesia and South Africa. Arnold Toynbee, who glowed when he shook Hitler's hand, called the displacement of Arabs by Israelis an atrocity greater than any committed by the Nazis.

Soviet Russia is an empire without a history. Its true history can be written only by its enemies. To the Soviets, Lenin is almost the only historical figure. Most of the other people who played leading roles in the rise of the Soviet empire have become non-persons. It is fantastic that the Marxist worship of history should have resulted in an abolition of history and a return to mythology.

Total haters are not good at predicting the future. Those who hated Germany wholeheartedly could not contemplate the emergence of a democratic Germany integrated with the West. So, too, wholehearted Jew-haters could not possibly foresee the birth of a puissant Israel that would defy a hundred million Arabs. Hence it might well be that my loathing of Russia prevents me from detecting signs of a new, civilized Russia taking shape in Brezhnev's spiritual wasteland.

131

May 24, 7:45 A.M.

It has been an article of faith since the French Revolution that nothing great can be accomplished without enthusiasm. Is it not possible to achieve the momentous in an unmomentous way? Surely an enterprising, skilled population should be able to do great things in a sober, workaday spirit. It has been said of the people who built Ford's first assembly line that to them work was play and that if it had not been play it would have killed them. One might say that the vigor of a society is proportionate to its ability to dispense with enthusiasm.

Righting wrongs does not increase social concord. Women's liberation, racial equality and the war on poverty have not made us a more united nation. On the contrary, social justice has multiplied grievances and fueled discord. Like total freedom, total justice may become a cause of social disintegration.

Civilized life is based on an acceptance of imperfection—on not trying to enforce every right one possesses.

It is the testimony of the ages that there is little happiness—least of all when we get what we want. Many outstanding persons who reviewed their lives in old age found that all their happy moments did not add up to a full day.

The entrance of the masses onto the stage of history has not produced the anarchy forecast by many social thinkers in the nineteenth century. Yet the fear of the masses persists. The reason is that the self-assertion of the masses is threatening the cultural elites. Where every mother's son feels competent to write or paint, being a writer or an artist is no longer the rare achievement it has been through all of history. To Robert Graves, "Writing has become almost meaningless as a descriptive term since popular education opened the dikes to a shallow sea." According to Marcel Duchamp, "When painting becomes so low that laymen talk about it, it doesn't interest me." Abstruseness and abstraction are probably devices to preserve a cultural monopoly.

May 25, 6:30 A.M.

Has there ever been a time when people felt, as they do now, that comes the big wind not much will be left of what is now touted as great? We see an unprecedented outdatedness overtaking cultural products. When cultural life is dominated by clowns, nothing lasts.

Modernization has everywhere weakened social cohesion by draining the traditional authorities of church and family of their effectiveness, and by discrediting long-established customs and attitudes. So far, the advanced countries have failed to evolve a durable new organizing principle of society. The mushrooming big cities characteristic of our age are a dumping ground of the debris of communal entities shattered by the march of progress. Nowhere has this human debris been integrated into new social bodies.

One can see the advantage Japan and probably other countries of the Chinese Far East have in the present social crisis. Japan's strong sense of identity and group solidarity enabled it to ward off the social disorganization which accompanied modernization elsewhere. The countries of the Chinese Far East know how to transplant ancient group values to new institutions. This is particularly true of the deeply rooted family relationships. Hence the Chinese Far East is becoming an ideal milieu for the development of esprit de corps—the formation of family ties among strangers—in neighborhoods, factories, offices, armies and so on.

The Greeks had no holy books, no received truths, no venerated classics, and no scientific or philosophical jargon. The speech of the uneducated was also the speech of the intellectuals. The Greeks had a lot to say and little to hide. They did not need obscurantist double-talk to cover up their emptiness or shame.

The ancient Hebrews were alone in their cultivation of compassion. The Bible forbids the muzzling of an ox in his threshing whereas the Romans muzzled slaves grinding grain. To the Greeks, too, slaves were not human.

It is a paradox that the Greeks, who invented individual freedom, were the first to institutionalize slavery. In the pre-Greek world all men were servile and chattel slavery was of minor importance. To the clear-thinking Greeks freedom meant freedom from the servitude of work.

The automated machinery of a post-industrial society is more than an effective equivalent of the slave population that did much of the work in classical Greece. But could a modern society match what the Greeks did with their freedom from work?

May 26, 9:30 A.M.

The silent majority has no hopes. It has fears: fear of inflation, fear of violence in the streets, fear of having houses and cars ransacked, fear of losing its children to the drug and drift culture. A party that aspires to become a party of the majority must address itself to these fears.

The Democratic party is increasingly becoming a party of the minorities. The question is whether the Republicans can develop the sweep and drive necessary to stir the majority and convince it that there are practical ways to cure its fears.

Leibnitz thanked God for placing Russia between China and Europe. I have to remind myself that until well into the nineteenth century Russia felt itself and was seen by others as a European country. The industrial revolution opened a gap between a modern West and a backward Asiatic Russia. Paradoxically, it was Western Marxism that made Russia murderously anti-Western.

In 1917 the Germans brought a plague-carrying rat in a sealed train to the edge of Russia and let it loose. The rat set off a ravaging pestilence that killed sixty million Russian men, women and children. No one knows whether the pestilence has burned itself out or is merely dormant.

When the rat died its body was embalmed and placed in a glass case. It is worshiped as a God in a temple in Moscow. There are many people in other countries who have been converted to rat worship.

May 27, 6:00 A.M.
      Slept fitfully. The left arm is giving me trouble. The first thought this morning was about my lack of a fruitful train of thought. The short essays I have been writing are links in a chain. I could combine several of them into larger chapters. But I hunger for a totally new train of thought to chew on.

It is blasphemous that a quadrupling of the price of oil by a bunch of crummy sheiks should drain the Occident of its dynamism and put to nought its vaunted uniqueness. How could greatness be so meek and brittle! Of what avail are the Occident's science and technology, its mastery over nature, and its feats of organization if a dozen unarmed tribal chieftains can bring it to its knees? Our cowardice is making a mockery of our proud past and grandiose aspirations. How could it be that in the whole of the proud Occident there is not at present one great leader who will declare the end of the fossil-fuel age, mobilize the Occident's know-how and ingenuity to produce a new, cheaper and cleaner fuel, and tell the oil sheiks to go drink their oil?

The mystery of our time is the inability of decent people to get angry. At present, anger and daring have become the monopoly of a band of mindless juvenile terrorists.

Social automatism is at its height when a society is engaged in a struggle to master nature. It is then that impersonal factors move people to action and the need for the deliberate management of men is minimal. But once things have been mastered and want is banished much of the social automatism disappears. A triumphant technology ushers in a psychological age, and history is made not by the hidden hand of circumstances but by men. For the mass of people the outcome of technological progress is a passage from servitude to things to the more demeaning servitude to men.

I used to think it self-evident that freedom means freedom from iron necessity. But it is not quite so. The moment necessity no longer regulates and disciplines there is need for imposed regimentation. On the other hand, a society living on the edge of subsistence cannot afford freedom. Thus the zone of individual freedom is midway between the extremes of scarcity and abundance.

May 28, 7:00 A.M.

The prospect for liberty in Russia is growing dimmer not because the men in the Kremlin are tightening their grip but because the system makes people unfit for freedom. Many of those who are allowed to leave Russia sooner or later feel abandoned and forgotten in a free society. The free individual strikes them as anarchic and the free society as chaotic.

Still, people continue to run from non-free to free countries rather than the other way around.

Does not civilized living depend on not seeing things as they are? There can be neither order nor stability and continuity without illusions about authority, about the attainability of desired goals, about the quality of our fellow men and about our own nature. A confrontation with naked, raw reality shreds the fiber of civilized life.

Is there nostalgia for colonial days among the people of the new African states? Liberation has meant a change from colonialism by white civil servants and soldiers to colonialism by black intellectuals and soldiers. White colonialism certainly was more efficient, honest and humane than the regimes of Amin, Mobutu or whatever their names.

I am reminded of the Slavonian longshoremen who spoke warmly of Austrian rule in Slovenia, Croatia and Dalmatia before the First World War. It was easygoing, civilized and honest; far preferable to Serbian rule which took its place.

May 29, 8:30 A.M.

My faith in America is partly faith in its digestive powers—its capacity to absorb and assimilate foreign bodies. During the past 150 years, whenever there was an influx of outsiders there were knowledgeable people who wondered whether the country could preserve its identity. In 1868 Sir Charles Dilke predicted that the Irish who were packing the cities would become America's new ruling class and the squeezed-out "law-abiding Saxons" a docile peasantry.

America is the worst place for alibis. Sooner or later the most solid alibi begins to sound hollow. Even the alibi of heredity becomes irrelevant. To come to America is to be reborn, to start with a clean slate. Here you are your own creator and your own ancestor.

In America nothing is finished. The social and political chemistry is still active. Everything is still in solution, and every reaction reversible.

America is the classic land of rebirth and new beginnings. You cannot predict the performance of an American from his past.

Jewish intellectuals in France: Henri Bergson wanted a Catholic priest to pray at his funeral. The historian Marc Bloch requested before his execution by the Nazis that Hebrew prayers *not* be said at his grave. For all we know, the reaction against their ancestry, against the ancient blood in their veins, may have been a factor in the creativeness of these two Jewish-

French intellectuals. One wonders how the miracle of Israel would have affected them.

4:15 P.M.   I met Jack Lurie outside the Safeway market near where I live. His face looked drawn. He is eighty-three years old and has been retired from the waterfront for fifteen years. His stomach is giving him trouble for the first time in his life and he is panicked. He also feels terribly alone—has no kin or close friends. All of a sudden he started to cry. I put my arms around him and tried to console him. I did not know what to say.

May 30, 7:20 A.M.
    I picked up yesterday a copy of the *Nation*, a magazine I have not touched in almost twenty years. It is curious how urbane and forbearing leftists are when they write about Russia. They become universalists. Russia's evil is but an aspect of the universal evil that afflicts humanity. Stalin's terror was a Russian version of McCarthyism. The persecution of dissidents is indicative of the intellectual's high standing in Soviet Russia. What the intellectual says and writes in Russia is of vital concern both to the government and the people, whereas in this country no one takes intellectuals seriously.
    The same people who denounce the least infringement of freedom in a democracy see the crimes of communism as mistakes or as the by-product of the siege mentality induced by Western hostility. What needs explaining is why this double standard has been adopted by people who are not radical but pride themselves on their sophistication. To judge Russia as we do other countries is seen by many as a mark of know-nothingness.

    At present, no matter how prosperous a free society might be it is still plagued by inflation, chronic unemployment and mindless violence. There is no reason to believe that copious new sources of fossil fuels and serviceable substitutes for scarce raw materials would change the situation. There is evidence on every hand that material resources are not as decisive as they used to be. Have we entered a new era in which old axioms are no longer valid? It might well be that at present advanced countries can remain free and stable only when they realize and utilize their human resources. Intractable problems would solve themselves once there was a wide distribution of work, a participation of common people in cultural pursuits, and unlimited opportunities for the young—from the age of ten—to acquire skills and become self-reliant.

Every era has a currency that buys souls. In some the currency is pride, in others it is hope, in still others it is a holy cause. There are of course times when hard cash will buy souls, and the remarkable thing is that such times are marked by civility, tolerance and the smooth working of everyday life. In Britain at present souls cannot be bought no matter what the currency, hence perhaps the sluggishness and confusion.

May 31, 6:30 A.M.
     My reconciliation with life as it is stems in no small part from the fact that in my lifetime millions of individuals more deserving and more richly endowed than I have died like rats in trenches, gas chambers and labor camps.

Modern history came to an end with Lenin's revolution. The Bolsheviks aspired to bring history to an end by eliminating classes. Instead they brought modern history to an end by eliminating individual freedom and initiative and the friendship, loyalty and honor which can mark the intercourse between autonomous individuals.

I am obsessed with what is going on in Britain—the precipitate decline of a country with unimpaired creative powers in literature, art, music, science, technology and agriculture. Lethargic businessmen and disillusioned workingmen are turning Britain into one of the lesser nations of Europe. It is weird to hear Harold Wilson plead with British manufacturers and workingmen not to let Britain fall out of the twentieth century.

How will it end? Socialism cannot induce the British worker to work harder. Nowhere has socialism energized the masses. Nor is there a leader or a movement in sight that could pull Britain out of its lethargy. We also know that gold will not make a difference. Should the flow of oil from the floor of the North Sea make Britain rich, she will become an Anglo-Saxon Saudi Arabia.

During the nineteenth century Britain was a fabulous swamp, heavy with stenches and perfumes. There were slums, palaces, loot from distant places, satanic mills belching sulfurous fumes, incredible riches, the finest parks and greenest lawns, surging poetry, momentous theories and discoveries. Now, in the last quarter of the twentieth century, the swamp is drained and the air is clear. There are no fabulous growths and no crawling things—just a manicured little island with a weary population intent on taking it easy and having modest fun.

It is more than six months since I started this diary. I wanted to find out whether the necessity to write something significant every day would revive my flagging alertness to the first, faint stirrings of new ideas. I also hoped that some new insight caught in flight might be the seed of a train of thought that could keep me going for years.

Did it work? The diary flows, reads well, and has something striking on almost every page. Here and there I suggest that a new idea could be the subject of a book; but only one topic, "the role of the human factor," gives me the feeling that I have bumped against something which is, perhaps, at the core of our present crisis.

From the early days of the industrial revolution, intellectuals of every sort predicted that the machine would make man redundant. Even now, most social scientists seem to believe that automated machines and computers are eliminating man as a factor in the social equation. It is an article of faith of the educated that the machine dehumanizes, stifles individuality, and turns men into slaves and robots; and this belief, not founded on experience or observation, is blinding social scientists to what is happening around them. It prevents them from realizing that the denouement of advanced technology is the opposite of what they anticipated. There is evidence on every hand that the human factor has never been more central than it is now in countries with automated economies. It is this centrality of the human factor which makes post-industrial society so unpredictable and explosive.

No one foresaw the startling consequences of a taste of limitless plenty made possible by a triumphant technology. We assumed that societies are shaped by traditions, beliefs, spiritual values and the like. How, then, could the trivial fact that people no longer have to work hard for a living cause a breakdown of age-old attitudes?

Actually, all through the millennia work has been the main theme of human existence. Society itself originated in the need for a concerted effort to wrest a livelihood from grudging nature. Work also was the chief source of a sense of usefulness, and the means by which the young proved their manhood. You became a man by doing a man's work and getting a man's pay. The battle against want mobilized and disciplined. It was the hidden hand of scarcity that regulated and managed men through most of history. In a world of scarcity, the innate anarchy of the human condition is kept locked in the dark cellars of the individual's psyche and is not allowed to inject its unpredictability into everyday life.

The nineteenth century, which was engaged in a Promethean effort to master nature, gave little thought to the management of men. The ruling middle classes proceeded on the principle that government is best when it governs least. Social affairs were so predictable that is was natural to believe in the possibility of a social science as rational and exact as the natural sciences. Walter Bagehot wrote a book on *Physics and Politics*. Despite the drastic changes brought about by the industrial revolution, everyday life in the nineteenth century was marked by a phenomenal orderliness and a sense of permanence. Millions of people went to work each morning and returned from work each evening "with a regularity akin to the moon's tide." Submission to law was prompt and sure as a reflex movement. There was also an unbounded hope—faith in progress—which unified and disciplined people.

Things began to change after the First World War. There was a loss of hope. Political chaos in Russia, Italy and Germany prepared the ground for dictatorships. In the Western democracies anarchic individualism gathered force during the upsurge of technological advance after the Second World War. The terrible 1960s were years of unprecedented abundance. From early 1961 to late 1969 this country's economy went through 106 months of unbroken prosperity. The anarchy released by this affluent decade has increased enormously the weight of the human factor in social calculations. The fear of youth exploding in the streets is often preventing governments from making the right decisions in both domestic and foreign affairs.

A further enhancement of the role of the human factor came with the exhaustion of raw materials and sources of energy by excessive industrialization. It is now clear that in the post-industrial age, human rather than natural resources are the wellspring of a nation's wealth, vigor and greatness. In order to survive at present a country must not only know how to cope with political anarchy but also how to develop and harness the ingenuity and creative talents of its people. Fortunately, by becoming creative a society is likely to tap a new source of social discipline. For the creative individual, no matter how richly endowed, cannot achieve much without hard work. A learning, creative society is automatically a disciplined society.

It stands to reason that the coming of the creative society will be slow and faltering. In the meantime, the chief task of a free society will be the preservation of the modicum of order and stability requisite for civilized living. Adversary influences will make this task particularly difficult. All through the diary I harp on the present impossibility of a strong government in free societies. The education explosion is producing a horde of nobodies who want to be somebodies and are prone to dramatize themselves by spectacular acts which disrupt the status quo. The absence of great leaders everywhere not only eliminates leadership as an effective instrument but also favors the appearance of "anti-leaders." For it seems that in a time unpropitious for the emergence of great leaders, incompetent nonentities suddenly see themselves as men of destiny, run for high office, and get elected.

The question is how to keep political anarchy free of mindless violence. Can this be done by popularizing, legitimizing, and routinizing social protest? If the silent majority could be induced to voice its grievances and find quick remedies by traditional procedures, the militant minorities could no longer dramatize themselves as vanguard, and would be left without an audience to impress and shock by spectacular acts of violence.